A CREWEL
EMBROIDERY PRIMER

A CREWEL
EMBROIDERY PRIMER

by Nancy O. Hobbs

TRIDENT PRESS  NEW YORK

For Nigel

SBN 671-27110-5
Library of Congress Catalog Card Number: 73-82871
Designed by Jack Jaget
Manufactured in the United States of America

1 2 3 4 5 6 7 8 9 10

Contents

Acknowledgments

I am very grateful to all my friends who so generously contributed their time, talents, and typewriters to the creation of this book. Special thanks to Renée and Percy Young, Cathy and Paul Nolan, Franco Basurto, Ann Freeman, Anne Tucker, Ellen and Mitch Silver, Barbara and Charles Morgan, and Emil Wurio, president of the DMC Corporation.

DMC products are available by mail from the catalogues of:

Merribee
2904 West Lancaster
P.O. Box 9680
Fort Worth, Texas 76107

Lee Wards
1200 St. Charles Road
Elgin, Illinois 60120

Chapter 1
Materials

Now that your interest has been sparked in what could be a new craft for you, the first thing you should do is familiarize yourself with the materials needed in the craft. This will aid you greatly in gaining the utmost satisfaction from your enthusiasm, energy, and ideas. In the case of crewel embroidery, four basic kinds of materials are necessary: needles, yarn, fabric, and a frame. Because of the current popularity of all types of needlecrafts, most of the materials should be readily available either in a department store or a needlework shop. (If not, there are two catalogues mentioned in the Acknowledgments to this book which are quite easy to obtain and which offer an excellent stock of needlework supplies.) Above all, you should not cut corners when purchasing materials for your projects. There is little logic in wasting valuable time in stitching a piece of embroidery if you use inferior materials, for it will not withstand the rigors of normal wear.

There are two types of needles you will need for your work: crewel, or embroidery, needles and tapestry needles. Crewel needles are sharp-pointed and are used for stitching when the yarn and needle constantly pass through the front and back sides of the fabric. They should be medium in length and have a long eye. The body of the needle should be slightly thicker than the yarn used for stitching, so that the

needle will open a pathway for the yarn to slip through easily. Otherwise the yarn will become fuzzy and could possibly break from the wear of passing back and forth through the resisting fabric. Tapestry needles have blunt points and are used to embroider stitches that are worked mainly on the surface of the fabric. In Chapter 2 you will find suggestions as to when to change from an embroidery to a tapestry needle. Ideally, the tapestry needle should never be passed through the fabric, because the blunt point sometimes splits the threads of the fabric and roughens the finish of the material. However, it becomes very troublesome to switch needles constantly, so for practical purposes, simply try to avoid passing the tapestry needle through the fabric more than is absolutely necessary.

Both crewel, or embroidery, needles and tapestry needles are usually sold in packages of assorted sizes. Crewel needles range in size from 10 to 1, the needles with higher numbers being finer than those with lower numbers. That is to say, a No. 8 needle is thinner and smaller than a No. 3 needle. The No. 5 needle will probably be the one you use most frequently; Nos. 3 and 4 are best for use with heavy yarn. For very fine woolwork use a No. 8, 9, or 10 needle. Tapestry needles range in size from 24 to 15. Just as with crewel needles, the higher-numbered tapestry needles are finer than the lower-numbered ones. A good average-size needle for use in embroidery is 21 or 22.

Before discussing crewel wool, we should clarify the meanings of four words that are used in connection with yarn: "strand," "ply," "thread," and "filament." Filaments, the most basic element, are the irregular-length wool fibers that are twisted together to form a single ply of wool. This single ply is not sufficiently strong, so it is then twisted together with at least one other ply to form a strand of yarn. The words "strand" and "thread" are often applied interchangeably to a piece of yarn used in crewel embroidery, but for the purpose of clarity, the word "strand" will be used exclusively throughout this book. In my opinion, use of the word "thread," which has the connotation of cotton, is confusing when applied to wool yarn.

Properly, crewel yarn has little elasticity and is two-ply; never untwist a strand of yarn in an attempt to embroider with a single ply. This yarn is most often sold in hanks, or skeins, of one ounce or of a specific number of yards. There is no hard-and-fast rule concerning the number of strands of yarn with which each stitch should be embroidered. Some stitches are in fact more appealing if they are worked with more than one strand of yarn, and others are more attractive when worked with a single strand of yarn. (Where this choice is applicable, it has been stated in the stitch instructions given in Chapter 2.)

However, my belief is that today's embroiderer, who does not have to weave her own cloth and dye her homemade wool, should take advantage of the products that are available to her. My suggestion is to experiment with wool that is heavier in weight and bulkier than crewel yarn (rug and tapestry wool, for example). Unique and interesting effects are achieved when bulky wool is used in combination with crewel wool in a piece of embroidery. Varying the thicknesses of yarn in your piece—either by using a different number of strands of crewel yarn or by introducing a different weight of yarn—is an excellent way to discover and to create new effects in embroidery.

Furthermore, many lovely pieces of embroidery have been stitched with a combination of crewel yarn and embroidery cotton floss or entirely in cotton thread. (Some women find that they prefer to work with cotton, especially during the summer months.) There are different weights and finishes to embroidery cotton thread, just as there are various weights of wool. The vast number and different types of threads that are marketed today can be overpowering if you have absolutely no idea of the usage and characteristics of each type. Below you will find a brief glossary of the types of cotton thread produced by the DMC Corporation which I hope will serve as a guide to you when you purchase embroidery cotton.

Six-strand embroidery thread: This is the thread most often used in embroidery. It is divisible into six strands and may be used singly or in any combination of threads. This cotton is available in a broad range of solid and shaded colors and combines nicely with other types of cotton thread or wool.

Four-strand mat-finish embroidery thread: This four-strand divisible cotton may also be used singly or in any combination of threads. The mat finish adds an exciting contrast to all pieces of embroidery, whether the thread is used in combination with wool or cotton. The colors available are very happy, bright shades.

Nondivisible mat-finish cotton thread: This nondivisible mat-finish thread is excellent for embroidery in which you would like to produce a bold effect in combination with a contrast in finishes. Available in a wide range of colors, this thread is very useful in wool and cotton work.

Pearl cotton: This thread has a soft, pearly finish and is available in four thicknesses—1, 3, 5, and 8. The finest thickness is size 8; the heaviest is size 1. Ideal for embroidery of all kinds, pearl cotton combines well with yarn to produce a very interesting effect. Of course, you may combine all thicknesses of pearl cotton in one piece of embroidery to vary the texture in another way. The color range is wide, both in solid and shaded colors.

The fabric on which crewel embroidery is worked should be of good quality and strong enough to withstand wear and stretching over a frame. The type of fabric you use depends largely on the nature of the project you are planning. A piece that will receive considerable wear, such as an armchair cover, footstool or chair-seat cover, should be worked on a heavy fabric, whereas a wall hanging, a picture, a mirror frame, or a pillow can be worked on a lighter-weight fabric. For these latter types of embroidery, Belgian linen has been the most commonly used fabric. However, with the increasing popularity of this art form, constant experimentation has expanded the range of embroidery fabrics to include Irish and less formal varieties of linen, burlap, all kinds of cotton, and wool. Increasingly, the ever-popular richer fabrics, such as velvet, satin and silk, are being decorated with embroidery stitches. I heartily encourage you to initiate some of your own ideas about fabric; trial and error is one of the best ways to discover innovative concepts in crewel embroidery.

One item used in crewel embroidery remains to be discussed: the frame. If you have ever considered an embroidery frame as a purposeless piece of equipment, erase that thought from your mind! Stitching with your fabric held tightly in a frame helps you to regulate and control the tension of your yarn and keep the stitches even and smooth. In addition, it will prevent a large proportion of wrinkles and enable you to work with both hands at the same time, which is an asset when you embroider. In some cases, the nature of a stitch demands that it be embroidered with the fabric held snugly in

a frame, because the stitch must be worked on a firm base; these instances are mentioned in Chapter 2. Clarity and distinctness are two important qualities of well-rendered stitches; a frame helps you to achieve this effect.

Embroidery frames are round and are sold in an assortment of sizes. The simplest frames are held in your lap; the other types have a supporting stand that leaves both hands free to pass the needle swiftly back and forth through the material—one hand below and the other above the frame. You may find it awkward at first to use both your right and left hands, but if you persevere and continue to pass the yarn up and down through the fabric from one hand to the other, you will find that using both hands becomes second nature.

There are four kinds of round frames: the ring frame; the ring frame with a table clamp; the lap, or table, frame; and the round frame with a floor stand. The ring frame consists of two round hoops, one slightly smaller than the other, which fit together. Usually these frames have a screw or clamp device that is adjustable to the thickness of your fabric. Available in wood or metal, ring frames range in diameter from four to ten inches. The most satisfactory ring frames are made of wood (because wood grips the fabric well) and have the screw type of adjustment. (This is easily regulated and imposes less wear on the fabric, especially if it is delicate.) The ring frame with a table clamp screws onto a table or the arm of a chair. The height and angle of this frame is adjustable. It is small enough to be taken anywhere as long as you can find a comfortable chair or table. The possible disadvantage of this frame is that you may not want to keep your work set up in the same place all the time. The lap or table frame has its own stand, which can, as the name implies, sit in your lap or on a table. The angle of working may be changed to satisfy your specific needs. Although the lap frame has the advantage of

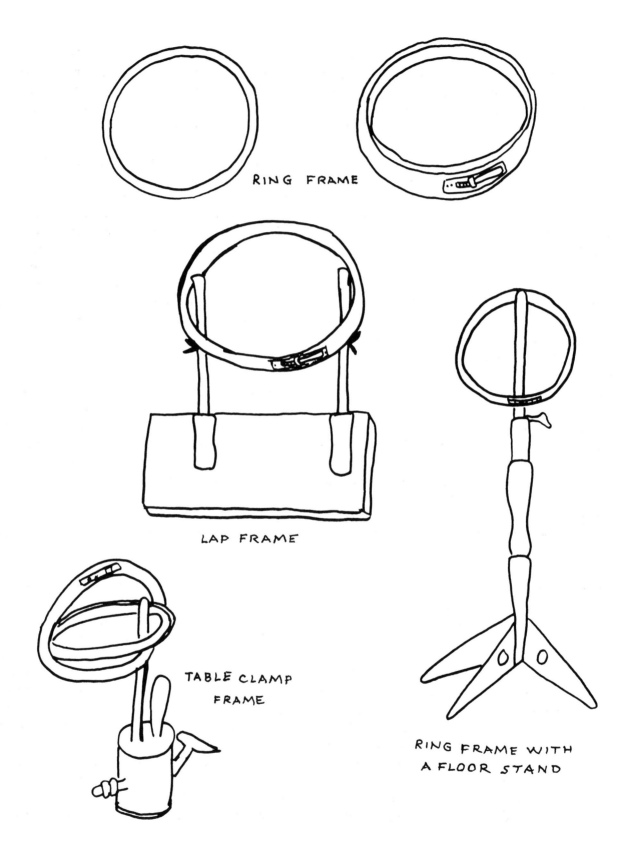

RING   FRAME

LAP FRAME

TABLE CLAMP
FRAME

RING FRAME WITH
A FLOOR STAND

being small enough to be portable, it may wobble occasionally when it is in use. The most sophisticated circular frame is the round frame with a floor stand. This frame is tall enough to stand directly on the floor and has adjustments for height and angle. If you are willing to make the investment, you will find this by far the most practical ring frame. While it is difficult to pack in a suitcase, the frame can easily be carried from room to room. You may also find it attractive as a piece of furniture. This round frame should have a base sturdy enough so that it does not wobble.

Whether you choose to start with a regular nine- or ten-inch ring frame or the grandmother of the round frames which has a floor stand, the procedure for setting the fabric in the frame is the same.

1. Separate the outer and the inner hoops of the frame.
2. Place the fabric over the inner ring (the smaller ring) of the frame, with the section of the design that you intend to embroider in the center of the hoop. By putting the design in the middle of the hoop you will be assured of having plenty of room to work.
3. Adjust the size of the outer ring so that it will fit snugly over the inner hoop and the fabric. Do this by tightening or loosening the screw at the opening in the outer hoop.
4. Having adjusted the outer hoop to the correct size, gently press the hoop around the circumference until it is in place. Pull the material tight as you push the outer ring over the inner ring. If you are embroidering a delicate fabric that might be marked by the rim of the frame, use tissue paper to protect the material. Put the tissue paper on top of the design and press the outer ring into position.
5. After you have completed step 4, cut away the tissue paper at the edges of the frame. This will enable you to embroider the design in the center of the hoop while the edges are safe from the pressure of the frame.
6. To dismantle the frame and remove the material, push the outer hoop away from the fabric and the inner hoop with your thumbs.
7. When you are ready to embroider another section of your design, repeat steps 1 through 4.

There is another device that you can use to hold your fabric taut—artist's strips, or stretcher strips. (They are referred to by either name.) When assembled, these strips form a square or rectangular frame that holds the whole piece tight. The embroidery fabric is attached to the back of the frame with tacks or staples and is then held in your lap to stitch. The individual pieces are sold in various lengths in art-supply stores and are very inexpensive. The disadvantages of this kind of frame are that it has no stand, and therefore both hands are not free to embroider at the same time, and that it can be used only once or for pieces that have identical dimensions. On the other hand, there is an advantage in having the entire piece of embroidery held tight in a frame at the same time, especially if your design is complicated.

Chapter 2
Illustrated Instructions for Stitching

Before you embark upon the pleasure of stitching you should become familiar with a number of simple but very important hints about working with embroidery, needles, yarn, and fabric. There is a proper way to begin and to end off your stitches, as well as a most efficient way to thread a needle. It is wise to take note of these hints so that you will be well prepared before making your first stitches. In addition, this will prevent the disappointing possibility of any piece you sew unraveling six months after you have completed your work.

The method of threading an embroidery or tapestry needle with yarn is quite different from threading a sewing needle with cotton thread. The embroidery needle is placed over the yarn rather than the yarn being inserted into the eye of the needle, which is the technique used to thread a needle to sew a hem.

Because these and all the instructions in this book were written with the right-handed embroiderer in mind, an apology is due to all left-handed embroiderers.

1. Holding the needle in your right hand and the yarn in your left hand, loop the yarn around the needle and grasp both ends of the yarn with your thumb and forefinger.

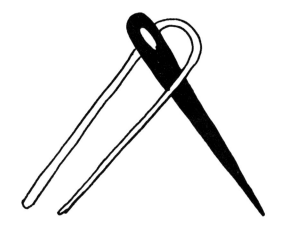

2. Tighten your grasp of the yarn slightly and slide your finger along the yarn until the yarn loop fits snugly around the needle.

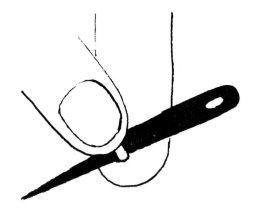

3. Squeezing the yarn, carefully slip the needle out of the now taut loop of yarn.
4. Continuing to hold the yarn between the forefinger and the thumb, place the eye of the needle over the yarn loop until a small amount of yarn "peeks" through the eye of the needle.

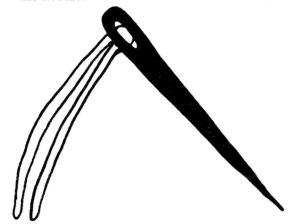

5. Pull the yarn through the eye.

Because most crewel pieces are usually backed, lined, or mounted, the appearance of the wrong side of your piece is not of great importance. Each time you start to sew with a new strand of yarn, make a knot at the end of the strand, as you would if you were using cotton thread to sew on a button. This knot will hold the yarn securely on the back side of the fabric while you embroider. To finish off your stitches, take a few small stitches on the back side of the fabric in a section of the design that you have just sewn. Take care not to allow long lengths of yarn to hang loosely from a knotted strand of yarn on ending off, or between one section of stitching and another. You will find that this practice helps make for uncomplicated stitching, because your yarn and needle will not get tangled in odd ends of yarn. Clip the ends of the yarn closely each time you end off. Secure your yarn between different stitching areas of a design either by taking two or three small stitches in a "safe" place (a space that will

later be covered with yarn) or by ending off and starting the new portion of the design with a fresh knot at the end of the strand.

Hold the needle close to the point as you stitch. This will give you more control over the needle in making precise stitches. You should stab the needle through the fabric, as opposed to sliding it in and out of the material, to ensure clarity of every stitch. Although all your stitches should blend together to enhance the over-all effect, this is accomplished only if each individual stitch is well defined. A stitch that is noticeably larger or smaller than the others in the same portion of a design can stick out painfully like a sore thumb, drawing the eye of your potential admirer to that very stitch rather than letting it glide across the whole work.

Before you begin stitching, examine your design to determine whether there are any sections that overlap each other. Any object that is covered by another should be worked first. The object that is on top or actively overlying the other should be sewn after the first one. For example, part of a butterfly's wing in a design might be obscured by a flower petal. The butterfly's wing or the overlapped object should be embroidered before the flower petal or the overlapping object is worked. By sewing the appropriate parts of a design in the proper order, a smoother effect is obtained, and no fabric will show through your stitching at overlapping points.

The selection and placement of the stitches in a design should be approached with care. Certain stitches are better suited to express a strong line, while others convey a delicate, soft appearance. An open, airy effect can be achieved in an object by using widely spaced stitches that do not totally cover the fabric. This category of stitches I shall designate as "open filling." Tightly packed stitches, or what I will term "close filling" stitches, give a forceful feeling to a piece. However, open filling stitches also double as effective border stitches, and most outline stitches are equally pretty when worked close together in a series of rows that conform to the shape of the object you are sewing. Very few stitches are confined to one type of use in a design; rather, they can be adapted to suit the embroiderer's whim. The chain stitch, for example, when worked in a series of adjacent rows is a close filling stitch, but becomes an effective border when large stitches are made. Commonly used open filling stitches include the cross stitch, the upright cross stitch, the star stitch, cloud filling, seeding, French knots, bullion knots, and the herringbone stitch. The Rumanian stitch, the satin stitch, long and short stitch, and the stem stitch may be used as closely worked filling stitches. The fun and challenge arises in learning the limitations and the versatility of each stitch and in skillfully combining each individual stitch with a compatible neighbor.

Balance the emphasis of each portion of your design by blending the different types of stitches that produce delicate and bold finishes. Simplicity should be your primary aim as you choose the stitches for your work. Using too many stitches in one piece tends to detract from the over-all effect of your embroidery. A tasteful combination of open and solid work and narrow and wide lines is a good goal. This is not meant to imply that using only one stitch or as many as twenty stitches in one piece is taboo, but it is wise to start out in a small way and increase the complexity of your stitch selection as your experience grows. Planning and experimenting will be the most effective means of acquiring skill in mixing the spicy and the soft stitches to produce an over-all pleasing effect.

A second balance must exist in your design —between the areas of the fabric that are completely stitched with yarn and those that are partially stitched and allow the fabric to show through. Of course, it must be left to individual preference to determine the exact amount of material left bare in any design. Some people want the texture and variety of crewel stitches to dominate their pieces and choose to stitch most of the fabric, while others prefer the effect produced by a balance of stitched and unstitched fabric. Experience and practice will aid in the process of making your own decision concerning the amount of fabric that is stitched and the balance that most accurately conveys the feeling of the design you are adapting to embroidery.

Varying the number of strands of yarn with which you sew one stitch is a simple method of acquiring a contrast of texture and strength in your pieces. What changes the look of a stitch is the variation in its size and the number of strands of yarn and the colors used to embroider. The gusto of French knots depends upon the use of one, two, or three strands of yarn. A firm line can be achieved by sewing two-strand stem stitches; a single-strand stem stitch produces a more moderate line. An interesting color effect is achieved when the variation in the number of strands of yarn is a combination of two colors or two shades of a color. This idea should be used in small doses, for it can overpower a piece of crewelwork.

Although there are fifty stitches described in the following pages, you should not be overwhelmed by this number for two reasons. First, the number of crewel stitches in existence could be said to be infinite, because the possible variations for each stitch are endless, without even considering the potential for the creation of new stitches. (Incidentally, the nomenclature and the steps involved in forming a stitch differ enough so that there can often be confusion in discussing the names of the stitches as well as the procedure in sewing a stitch.) Secondly, a large proportion of crewel stitches are related to one another or form the basis for two or three different stitches. Many of these stitches take on an entirely changed character when they are threaded with a different color of yarn, and yet they are sewn in the same fashion. The threaded herringbone stitch is essentially the herringbone stitch interlaced with a contrasting color of yarn. The herringbone stitch itself is a variation of the cross stitch, and it is much easier to work when this is understood.

To my mind, the most logical classification of crewel embroidery stitches is according to their common denominators. In some instances, one particular stitch is the basis for a number of other stitches. In other cases, the stitches are a sophistication of a basic stitch and are fashioned according to the same principle. This is the reason I have classified the stitches into nine categories: running stitches, back stitches, straight stitches, chain stitches, loop stitches, knotted stitches, cross stitches, woven stitches, and couched stitches. The basic stitch is illustrated and explained first and is most often a very simple stitch. Start at the beginning of every section and progress to the end. Although most stitches can be worked equally well with or without a frame, frames are an imperative piece of equipment with specific stitches. When this is so, it is noted in the instructions.

The Running Stitches

RUNNING STITCH

One of the most basic stitches of embroidery, the running stitch forms a dotted, or broken, line on both the front and back of the fabric. Normally the stitches are of equal size both front and back. However, a slight modification may be introduced by increasing or decreasing the length of the stitch on the back side of the fabric. This alters the spacing of the stitch on the front of the material. Whatever the variation, the stitches must be consistent. One, two,

or three strands of yarn may be used for this very good outline stitch.

1. Draw the needle and the yarn through the fabric at point A.
2. Pierce the fabric at point B; pull the yarn through to the back of the fabric.
3. Bring the needle back to the surface of the material at point C. The distance between points B and C should be the same distance as that between points A and B. Draw the yarn through the fabric.

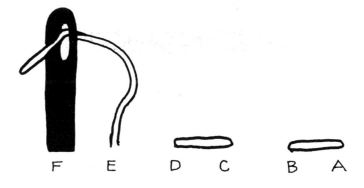

F   E   D   C   B   A

4. Continue in the same fashion to the end of the row.

DOUBLE RUNNING STITCH

This version of the running stitch is often used to express a solid line. The double running stitch is merely two rows of the running stitch pushed together into one row to become a solid line. One row of the simple running stitch is worked from the right to the left, and one row of the simple running stitch is then worked in the empty spaces from left to right. This stitch lends itself very well to the use of two colors—a different one in each direction. The effect is a two-colored line, which becomes an even more interesting border or filler if the colors are reversed in another row placed next to the first. One or two strands of yarn are best used with this stitch.

1. Work a row of running stitches (as explained on the previous page) from right to left.
2. Turn your piece of embroidery upside down and work a second row of running stitches between the stitches of the first row.

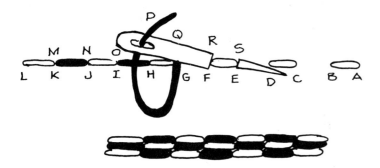

WHIPPED RUNNING STITCH

The whipped running stitch is a fanciful variety of the running stitch. To create this effect a strand of yarn is laced between the simple running stitches and the fabric. Two strands of yarn work very well when whipped with one strand of yarn. A heavier line may be produced by increasing the number of strands used for the foundation stitches, but make certain that the foundation stitches are always heavier than the whipping. Color shading and contrasting can be especially appealing in this stitch. One small hint: use a tapestry needle to whip the stitches.

1. Work a row of simple running stitches.
2. Bring the needle threaded with a contrasting or shaded color of yarn through the fabric at point A, underneath stitch 1. Remove the embroidery needle and thread a tapestry needle with the yarn.

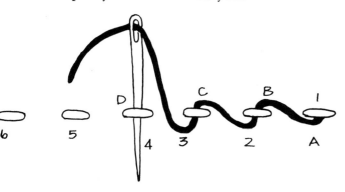

3. Place the needle perpendicular to stitch 2 and between the fabric and the stitch. Gently pull the yarn so that it lies naturally on top of the fabric.
4. Continue placing the needle between the fabric and the running stitches to the end of the row. End off the row on the back of the fabric underneath the last running stitch.

DOUBLE-THREADED RUNNING STITCH

Still another variety of running stitch, the double-threaded running stitch, is a charming border or line stitch when given enough room to show itself off. In addition, a unique texture is obtained if two or more rows are worked beside one another. As with the whipped running stitch, the most pleasing effect is achieved when the basic running stitches are worked with one more strand of yarn than the threading. Depending upon the size of the running stitches, generally one or two strands of yarn of a different color are suggested for the threading.

1. Work a row of simple running stitches.
2. Draw the needle and the yarn through the fabric behind stitch 1. Rethread the yarn into a tapestry needle.

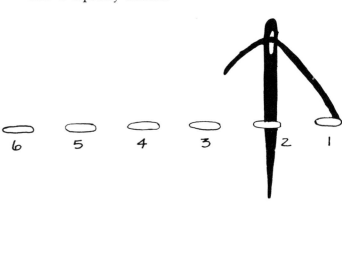

3. Place the needle perpendicular to stitch 2 on top of the material, as you did when whipping the running stitches. Again pull the yarn gently through the stitch, allowing the yarn to lie gracefully on the fabric in a half circle.

4. Turn the needle upside down and thread stitch 3 from the bottom, being careful to form a half circle with the yarn. Repeat steps 1 and 2 to the end of the row.

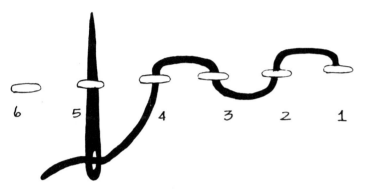

5. At the end of the row pierce the fabric behind the last stitch to be threaded. Continue pulling the yarn gently or you will lose the effect. End off on the back side of the material.

6. Draw the yarn through the fabric to the front side behind the last stitch (stitch 6) and thread the stitches in reverse order, but in the same manner as in steps 3 and 4, forming the second half of the circle.

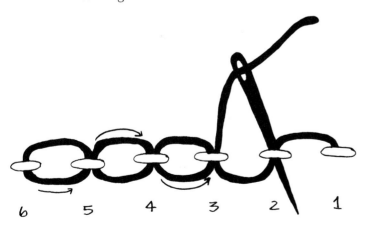

The Back Stitches

BACK STITCH

Since the back stitch makes a solid line when it is worked, it is very useful in outlining and lettering. It is also an innovative addition to other stitches, such as the chain stitch, which is discussed later in this chapter. Any number of strands of yarn may be used. Try combining two shades of a color for a simple border or filler. This stitch is quite flexible and can be used for lines in nearly all directions.

1. Bring the needle through the fabric at point A. Draw the yarn after it.

2. Put the needle through the fabric to the back of the piece at point B, a short distance away from point A. Bring the needle to the front side of the fabric at point C. The distance between points A and C should be the same as the distance between points A and B. Pull the yarn through to the front side.

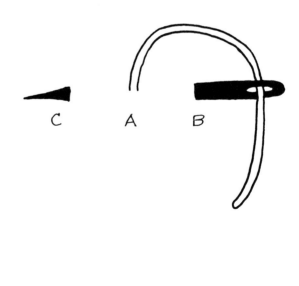

3. Insert the needle again back at point A and come out at point D. The distance between points C and D should equal the length of stitch AB.

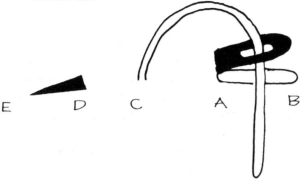

4. Repeat step 3, going back to point C and coming out at point E, until the row is completed. The finished stitches should resemble this illustration.

THREADED BACK STITCH

As in interlacing the running stitch, threading the back stitch with a color of yarn that contrasts with the color of the foundation stitches yields a distinctive line, border, or filling. The result is very special when no more than two threads are used to thread the back stitches. To prevent an accident and to facilitate threading, a tapestry needle should be introduced when the threading step begins. As shown in the illustration, the back stitch may be threaded in two directions, similar to the double-threaded running stitch.

1. Sew a row of back stitch.

2. Bring the needle up at point A, behind stitch 1.

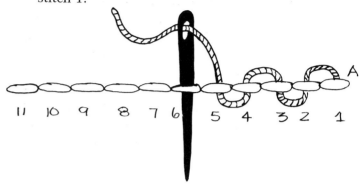

3. Using a tapestry needle, slide the needle between stitch 2 and the fabric; the needle should be perpendicular to the stitch. See above illustration. Pull the yarn carefully through the fabric to form a half circle between stitches 1 and 2.

4. Turn the needle upside down and again slide it between the fabric and stitch 3. Gently draw the yarn through the fabric until it lies in a half circle on the material.

5. Repeat steps 3 and 4 to the end of the row, ending off at the last stitch on the back side of the material.

6. As I suggested above, the threaded back stitch may be altered by double threading. The procedure is the same as with single threading except that the stitches are now threaded in the reverse order. That is to say, begin at stitch 10 and point the needle up between stitch 9 and the fabric and down between stitch 8 and the fabric. End off on the back of the fabric close to point A.

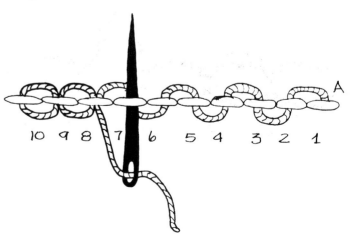

SPLIT STITCH

As the name implies, the split stitch is pierced, or split, in the center to form the neighboring stitch. A lovely filling stitch when placed in close rows and worked in one direction, this stitch adapts well to most shapes. Frequently the satin and long and short stitches are padded underneath with the split stitch. As padding, the split stitch is most successful when worked with one strand of yarn. When it is on its own, any number of strands of yarn may be found workable. Whatever the purpose, bear in mind one thing about this stitch: a frame is an ever-so-helpful aid in producing even stitches.

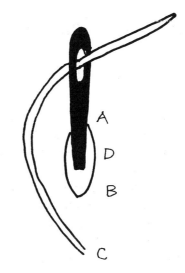

1. Draw the needle and the yarn to the front side of the fabric at point A. Insert the needle at point B to form the first stitch to be split (AB). Return the needle to the surface of the fabric at point C. The distance between points B and C should be half the length of stitch AB.

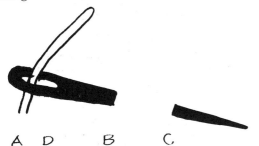

2. Stab the needle directly into point D, the middle of stitch AB, passing through the stitch and the fabric at the same time. See the illustrations of both the side and top views of this step.

3. Return the needle to the front of the fabric at point E. The distance between points C and E should be equal to that between points B and C.

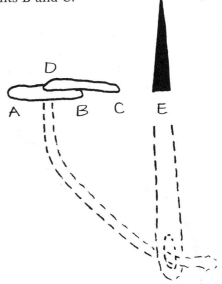

4. Repeat steps 1 and 2 to attain the finished product, as pictured.

The Straight Stitches

STRAIGHT STITCH

This very basic and almost-effortless-to-embroider stitch is so flexible that it can be worked freely in any and all directions. It is simply a straight line when it is completed. Attractive one-line designs become distinctive pillow patterns or unusual filling stitches (when treated on a smaller scale) if they are embroidered in the straight stitch. There are no bounds to the geometric configurations that can be sewn in this stitch, either scattered or organized into parallel rows. Extremely versatile (as you will see from the modifications that follow), the straight stitch can be worked with any number of strands of yarn.

1. Bring the needle and yarn to the front side of the material at point A. Return to the back side of the fabric at point B and come up again to the front side at point C.

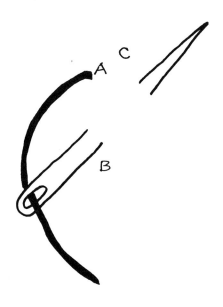

2. Insert the needle at point D and come up at point E.

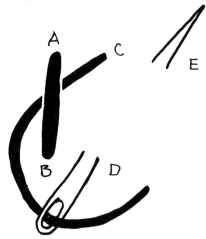

3. Continue to place the straight stitches in any design.

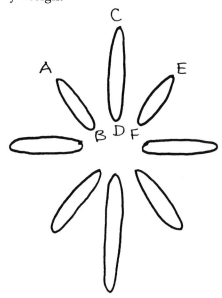

SEEDING STITCH

Because it is essentially two small stitches made almost on top of each other, the seeding stitch is what may be termed a "relief" stitch, since it projects above the level of the material.

The most effective placement of seeding is in small or large clusters as an open filling stitch. It almost gives life to an apple or a cherry when scattered heavily around the outer edges and lightly in the center. Flowers, leaves, butterflies' wings and ladies' dresses are among the myriad subjects to which seeding has been very attractively applied. The number of strands of yarn used depends upon how much or little body texture is desired. Above all, do not lose the effect by pulling the yarn tight. One strand of yarn gives a delicate shading to a subject; two or three strands add a stronger tone.

1. Come to the front side of the fabric at point A. Draw the yarn through. Insert the needle at point B, a tiny distance from point A. Remember that this illustration has been enlarged to demonstrate the stitch more clearly.

2. Return to the front side of the fabric at point A, preparing to work another stitch almost on top of stitch AB. Insert the needle at point C, near to but not exactly overlying point B.

3. Continue to make seeding stitches as explained in steps 1 and 2 until you have "sewn enough seeds" to your satisfaction. (Bad joke—although I'm told the worse they are, the better.) The finished effects are pictured in these three illustrations.

SATIN STITCH

A series of tightly packed straight stitches, the satin stitch is solely a close filling stitch. You will probably need to practice to produce the smooth and neat look that should be achieved with this stitch. (The sampler is an excellent means to this end.) In selecting objects to be worked with the satin stitch, bear in mind that they should not be too large. A large space filled with the satin stitch will not wear well, because the threads are apt to pull loose. Ragged yarn ends will hang free and muss your whole piece. Although the satin stitch can be worked successfully with two strands of yarn, you are well advised to acquaint yourself with the limitations of this stitch by first working it with one strand. The split stitch is used as padding around the outline of the object to be worked in the satin stitch. The padding not only raises the satin stitches slightly but also helps you to maintain a sharp edge. A frame is very much in order here.

1. Outline the shape to be worked with the satin stitch in the split stitch (page 19).

2. Bring the needle to the front side of the fabric at the bottom of the shape, outside and right next to the split-stitch padding, at point A. Pull the yarn through to the front. Stab the needle to the back side of the fabric at point B, directly across from point A. Pull the yarn to the back. Return the needle to the surface next to point A, at

point C. Although the needle is shown sliding through the fabric, be sure to insert it perpendicular to the fabric close to the split-stitch padding each time. The needle is drawn sewing through the material to illustrate the proximity of the stitches.

3. Insert the needle at point D, again outside the padding and next to point B, so that no fabric shows between stitch AB and stitch CD. Bring the needle to the front side of the fabric at point E, outside the padding and next to point C.

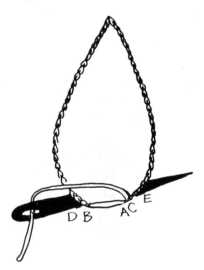

4. Continue in this manner until the entire space is filled.

WHIPPED SATIN STITCH

Whipping the satin stitch adds extra shading as well as relief to the basic stitch. To be effective the foundation stitches should be slanted and whipped almost at a right angle in a contrasting or complementary color. The most frequent use of this stitch is for leaves and flower petals, but there are any number of other shapes that can be worked in the whipped satin stitch. Like the satin stitch, the whipped satin stitch should not be stitched in too large a space, because of the risk of the whipping strands' being pulled loose. It is essential that you work this stitch in a frame.

1. Outline the shape in the split stitch (page 19).

2. In order to ensure that the slant of the foundation stitches is even, make the first stitch at the center of the shape. Bring the needle to the surface at point A, outside the split stitch padding, and pull the yarn to the surface of the fabric. Return the needle to the back of the fabric at point B, diagonally across from point A, outside the split stitch outline. Pull the yarn to the surface of the fabric.

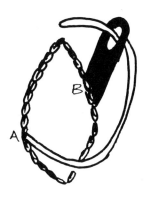

3. Bring the needle to the surface at point C, beside point A, and pull the yarn through. Continue working in slanting stitches to the top of the shape.

4. To fill the bottom half of the shape, bring the needle to the surface of the fabric at the center of the shape beside stitch AB at point E. Complete this stitch by inserting the needle at point F, beside and below point B, and pull the yarn through. Continue in this way until the remaining half of the shape is stitched. End off by weaving the yarn into previous stitches.

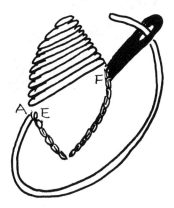

5. *Note*: To maintain the neat edge around your shape, try to insert the whipping yarn as near as possible to the holes that you used to work the foundation stitches. Bring the needle to the surface of the fabric at point G, slightly below the top of the shape. Pull the yarn to the surface of the embroidery. Insert the needle at point H, and return the

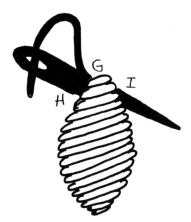

needle to the surface at point I. Pull the yarn through, being certain not to pull it too tight or the stitch will be distorted. Continue in this manner until the whipping is completed.

6. To end off, insert the needle at point J, return the needle to the back of the material after the last stitch is complete, and end off by again weaving the end into previous stitches.

SHEAF FILLING STITCH

A novel open filling stitch, the sheaf filling stitch is three tightly packed vertical straight stitches held together around the middle. A very original open filling stitch when scattered within a space or placed in neat brickworklike rows, this stitch also provides an interesting border when placed one next to the other. A frame facilitates your efforts to keep the straight stitches the same length. The sheaf filling stitch is most attractively displayed if it is worked with at least two strands of yarn.

1. Working from right to left, begin by making three straight stitches next to one another. Bring the needle to the surface at point A. Pull the yarn through. Return the needle to the back side of the embroidery fabric at point B. Pull the yarn to the back.

2. Bring the needle to the surface of the fabric at point C, to the left but quite close to point A. Draw the yarn to the front of the embroidery. Return the yarn to the back of the material at point D, beside point B, as shown. Pull the yarn through.

3. Make the third straight stitch, EF, to the left of stitch CD and return the needle to the surface underneath stitch EF—midway between the two points, so that the yarn emerges on the left of all three straight stitches.

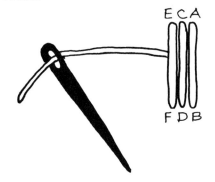

4. Slide the needle between the straight stitches and the surface of the fabric, as pictured. Pull the yarn through to the left and slide the needle a second time between the straight stitches and the surface of the fabric. Pass the needle and the yarn to the back side of the material underneath stitch CD and begin the second stitch as in step 1.

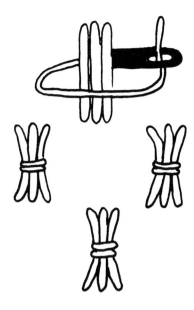

CLOUD FILLING

One of my favorite open filling stitches, cloud filling adds a lightness to any piece of embroidery. It is formed by threading a single strand of yarn through a series of strategically spaced tiny straight stitches. These foundation stitches should be worked with two strands of yarn. The size of the space is fairly flexible because the threading is anchored by the tiny stitches. Here is an opportunity to experiment with contrasting and shading colors, since this stitch is at its best when worked with different colors. A frame is essential.

1. Fill the space to be worked with short, straight stitches of equal size in a brickwork-like pattern. Work the stitches across the width of the space. The stitches of the second row should be placed between the stitches of the first row; place the stitches of the third row in line with those in the first row. Continue in this fashion until you have completed the number of rows of stitches you require to fill the space. The stitches of the odd-numbered rows (1, 3, 5, etc.) should form parallel lines, and the stitches of the even-numbered rows (2, 4, 6, etc.) should do the same.

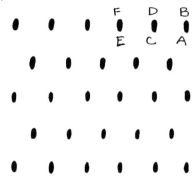

2. Draw a needle threaded with a single strand of contrasting yarn through the fabric under stitch A. Thread a tapestry needle with the yarn and slip the needle between stitch A and the material and down to stitch B. Slip the needle through stitch B and the fabric. Gently pull the interlacing yarn through these two stitches, permitting it to fall gracefully and naturally against the fabric. Following the direction of the arrows in the illustration, continue threading the yarn between the fabric and stitches C, D, E, F, G, H, I, J, and K. Insert the needle through the fabric to the wrong side and end off the row.

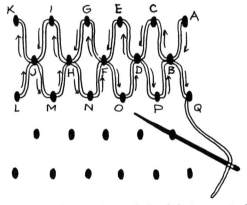

3. Come up to the surface of the fabric at stitch L, drawing the yarn again between the stitch and the material. Go up to stitch J and slip the needle between the stitch and the fabric, down and between stitch M and the fabric, and up and between stitch H and the fabric.

Continue threading stitches N, F, O, D, P, B, and Q in the direction of the arrows in the illustration. End off at stitch **Q**. Lace the remaining rows of foundation stitches.

LONG AND SHORT STITCH

Always a solid filler, the long and short stitch offers the opportunity to blend shades of color that few other embroidery stitches can match. In fact the colors seem to merge together in that the first row of stitches is worked in one color and forms an even border to the shape being filled, while the subsequent rows, which are worked in different tones of color, merge together to give the effect of soft shading rather than sharp contrast. Individual motifs as well as entire designs are equally adaptable to the long and short stitch.

In its simplest form, the long and short stitch has two stages: the first row and the succeeding rows. The stitches in the first row are of two different sizes, one being three quarters of the length of the other, worked side by side. In this row, the long stitches and the short stitches should be of regular length. The second and succeeding rows consist of equal-sized stitches worked over the first row, alternating up and down to continue the pattern. In these rows, uniform length should also be maintained.

Consistent tension in all your stitches is essential and may require practice. The rewards are well worth your time. To assure the needed clarity of each individual stitch, work the long and short stitch in a frame. Take special care to stab the needle straight into the fabric every time you stitch.

When you actually begin to work the stitch within a shape, you will have to adjust the stitch size to fit within the contours of the particular shape, especially when completing the final rows. In designs which include fanlike shapes or radiating shapes, such as a sun, you will find that as you work toward the center of the shape, you will also have to decrease the number and the size of the stitches. It is advisable to make the first stitch in the first row of arc-shaped designs (rainbows and flower petals, for example) in the center of the arc and work toward either edge, adjusting the angle of the stitches to fit within the arc. You may also have to wedge a few small short stitches very close to the regular length stitches (so that the wedge stitches barely show) to maintain the shape. In subsequent rows, you will then have to skip a stitch every now and then to continue the lines of the shape.

In addition to providing a padding, working the outline of the shape with the split stitch ensures that the edges will be neat and sharp. Usually the first row of long and short stitches will cover the split stitch padding. However, in stitching a circular shape, the first row of stitches will cover the split stitches, but with most shapes, part of the outline will remain exposed until the last stitches have been worked. At this point, as explained previously, you will have to alter the size of the stitches.

In most cases, the direction in which you should work the stitches is quite clear—that is, follow the natural flow of the shape. For example, in a leaf pattern, stitch in the direction of the leaf's tracery and you will achieve a beautiful result.

1. Outline the shape with the split stitch (page 19).

2. Bring the needle up at point A. The distance between point A and the split stitch outline should be the planned size of the long stitch. Insert the needle at point B, outside the split stitch and directly in line with point A. Stab the needle to the front side of the fabric at point C, which should be three-quarters of the length of stitch AB.

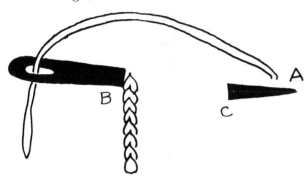

3. Complete the second and shorter straight stitch by inserting the needle at point D, beside point B and outside the split-stitch padding. Begin the third stitch (a long stitch) by returning the needle to the front side of the fabric at point E, fractionally below the level of stitch CD. All the long stitches should be the same length and all the short stitches should be the same length.

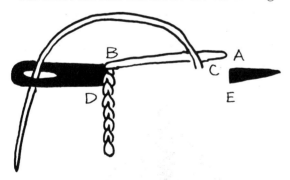

4. Continue making the long and short stitches to the desired number.

5. The second row and all additional rows of stitches are to be of equal length, although they appear to be long and short stitches because they fit into the gaps left by the first row of stitches. The second row marks the beginning of the shading. Each succeeding row may be worked in another shade of the main color. Come up at point A in the illustration, splitting stitch 1 approximately one-quarter of the way from the top. Insert the needle at point B.

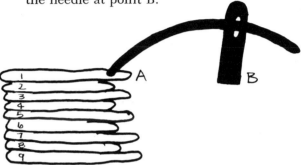

6. Stab the needle to the front side of the fabric at point C, about one-quarter of the distance from the end of stitch 2, as pictured. Complete stitch CD by inserting the needle at point D. Stitches CD and AB should be the same size.

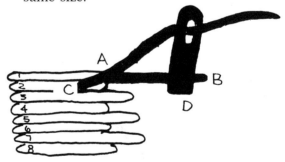

7. Continue to work the row and all additional rows in this manner. The illustration below shows the final effect.

The Chain Stitches

CHAIN STITCH

The chain stitch, resembling links of chain in its finished form, is created by drawing the needle through the loop of yarn that emerges from a previous stitch. One of the most readily mobile stitches, the chain can be worked in various directions. The constant recurrence of the chain stitch in Indian embroidery attests to its flexibility. As a close filling stitch, rows of the chain stitch can be placed side by side. However, there are two things that must be considered if you plan to use the stitch in this way: the size of each link and the number of strands of yarn. Using too many strands of yarn with a small link can spoil the look of the stitch. In fact, the stitch can resemble two short fat lines rather than a circular link if worked incorrectly. While this is not a difficult stitch to work, you would do well to experiment with different sizes and strands of yarn if you plan to use it as a close filling stitch. Outlines, borders, lines, and bands may all be successfully worked in the chain stitch too.

1. Draw the needle to the front side of the fabric at point A. Pull the yarn through as well. Form a loop toward the right and hold it down with your left thumb.

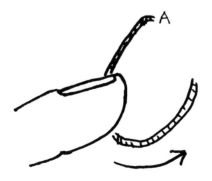

2. Insert the needle again at point A and bring it up to the front side of the fabric at point B. Keep the yarn loop underneath the point of the needle. Pull the needle and yarn through the loop until it lies flat against the fabric. Do not tug too hard on the yarn or there will be no link at all.

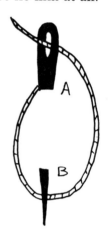

3. Form a loop to the right, as you did in step 1. Hold it down with your left thumb. Insert the needle again at point B, now inside the first link, and come to the surface of the material at point C. The distance between points B and C should be the same as the distance between points A and B, for this determines the size of the stitch. As you come out to the surface point C, keep the loop of yarn underneath the needle. Draw the needle and the yarn through the loop until it forms the second link.

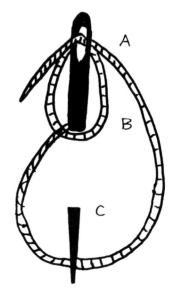

4. Repeat this process until you have made the desired number of stitches. Anchor the last stitch by taking a tiny straight stitch over the last link very close to the point inside the link from which you had previously been forming new stitches.

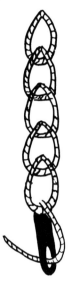

5. If you run out of yarn in the middle of a row of chain stitches and want to finish the row without losing the continuity of the stitch, do not tack the last link down as you would at the end of a row. Instead, let the last link hang free on the surface of the fabric, as

pictured. To do this, make a loop to the right and insert the needle at point A, but do not bring the needle to the surface. Weave the end of the strand into the previous stitches on the back of the piece. Draw the new strand to the front of the fabric inside the

free link (which you should be holding down with your left thumb) at point B, approximately the same distance away from the previous stitch as all the other stitches in the row. Pull the yarn through to the front of the fabric. Tighten the free loop by gently pulling the woven end of the yarn on the back of the material. Continue to make chain stitches to the end of the row by making a loop ahead, inserting the needle at point B, and coming out at point C, inside the loop, as pictured.

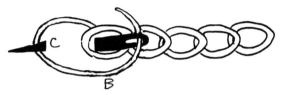

BACK-STITCHED CHAIN STITCH

Best worked as a border or in rows as a filling stitch, the back-stitched chain stitch is merely a row of chain stitches with a row of back stitches worked in the center of the links. This stitch is most effective when its composites are worked in contrasting colors. Be certain to make the chain stitches large enough to allow sufficient space in the center of each link to embroider the back stitch. If the links are too small, there will be no distinction between the two types of stitches and the quality of the entire stitch will be lost. Any number of strands of yarn may be used, providing you heed the previous suggestion.

1. Work a row of chain stitches, as explained previously in the section on chain stitches.
2. Draw a needle threaded with a contrasting color of yarn to the front of the fabric in the

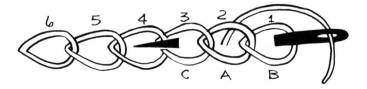

middle of stitch 2. Return the needle to the back of the fabric at point B, in the center of stitch 1. This forms the first back stitch. Come out at point C, in the middle of stitch 3.

3. Insert the needle at point A in stitch 2 and come out again at point D, in the center of stitch 4.

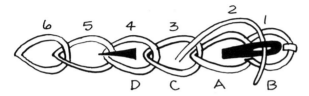

4. Continue in this manner until all the chain stitches are back-stitched.

WHIPPED CHAIN STITCH

This attractive modification of the basic chain stitch is most frequently used for borders, lines, and outlines. The stitch consists of a row of chain stitches whipped with a matching or contrasting color of yarn. The whipping falls over the juncture of each chain stitch, leaving the links showing. Usually, the most effectively whipped chain stitches are those whipped with the same number of strands of yarn as used for the foundation stitches. However, do not hesitate to experiment with different thicknesses of yarn to suit your own taste and purposes. The whipping is most conveniently done with a tapestry needle.

1. Begin by stitching a row of chain stitches as explained in the section concerning this stitch (page 28).

2. Bring the needle and yarn to the front of the piece at point A, as shown. Rethread the yarn into a tapestry needle.

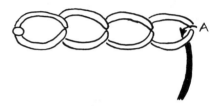

3. Place the needle in a vertical position between the fabric and stitch 2 and pull the yarn through until the yarn falls across the juncture of stitches 1 and 2.

4. Continue until the end of the row in the same manner, always sliding the needle between the fabric and the stitches from the same direction.

5. When you finish the row, remove the tapestry needle and thread the yarn into an embroidery needle. Insert the needle at point B as shown and draw the yarn to the back side of the material. End off in the usual manner.

CHECKERED CHAIN STITCH

The effect of the checkered chain stitch is quite unique in that it is a series of interlocking chain links of contrasting colors which give the appearance of having been embroidered at different times. Nonetheless, the entire row is embroidered at the same time. This is accomplished by threading a needle with two different-colored strands of yarn and slipping one strand over the point of the needle at the correct moment. This is a very versatile stitch and may be used as often as the basic chain stitch, as long as the color scheme is compatible with the coloring of the design that is being worked.

1. Begin by threading the needle with two strands of yarn of contrasting colors. For reasons of clarity, we shall speak about the black and the white strands of yarn in this example.
2. Draw the needle to the surface of the material at point A and form a loop to the right with both strands of yarn, as shown. Hold the loop down with the thumb of your left hand.

3. Insert the needle again at point A and return the needle to the surface at point B, without pulling the entire strand of yarn to the surface, and keeping the yarn loop underneath the needle point.

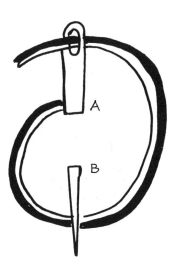

4. Just before you pull the needle and yarn to the surface, slip the black yarn over the needle point and let it lie on top of the needle. Pull the yarn through to the surface.

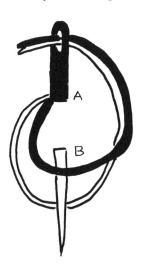

5. Form a loop counterclockwise as you did in step 2, and hold it in place with your left thumb. Insert the needle again at point B, now inside the link, and return the needle to the surface at point C without pulling the entire strand of yarn to the surface. The length of stitch BC should be the same as that of stitch AB, in that these stitches determine the size of the checkered chain stitch.

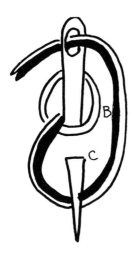

6. This time, slip the white yarn off the needle point and let it lie on top of the needle. Pull the yarn and needle to the surface of the fabric.

7. Continue in the same fashion to the end of the row, slipping the black yarn over the needle point to make the third stitch in the row and the white yarn for the fourth stitch. You might also try establishing different patterns—two white stitches and two black stitches, for example, or three white stitches and one black stitch. There are many combinations.

8. To finish the final stitch in the row, make a small tack stitch over the last link as shown. If at any time you are making a stitch of one color and there is a bit of yarn of the other color showing on the surface of the fabric from the previous stitch, a gentle pull on the errant strand of yarn will rectify the situation.

ROSETTE CHAIN STITCH

Best stitched relatively small and close, the rosette chain stitch is quite effective as either a line stitch, a border, or a floral motif when worked in a small circle. It is worked from right to left with any number of strands of yarn. The easiest way to keep the size of the stitches uniform and in a straight line is to imagine that two parallel lines run across the section in which you intend to use this stitch. If you are working in a circle, then your imaginary lines will, of course, become concentric circles.

1. Remembering to work from right to left, bring the needle and yarn to the front surface of the fabric at point A along the top imaginary parallel line, as shown. Make a loop to the right and hold the loop in place with your left thumb.

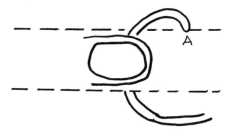

2. Insert the needle at point B, a little below and slightly to the left of point A. Return the needle to the surface at point C, on the lower imaginary line, on a diagonal from point B. Keep the loop underneath the needle. Pull the yarn through to the surface of the fabric.

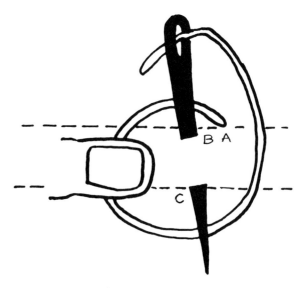

Detail of a wool embroidered curtain made in England circa 1729. Crown Copyright, Victoria and Albert Museum, London.

This is an English sampler signed by Mary Pether and dated 1839. Crown copyright, Victoria and Albert Museum, London.

Stitched in England during the second half of the 17th century, this bed curtain is worked in stem stitch, chain stitch, back stitch, and knotted chain or link stitch. Courtesy of Victoria and Albert Museum, London. Photograph by Sally Chappell.

Part of an English bed curtain made during the late 17th century stitched in satin stitch, stem stitch, and long and short stitch. Courtesy of Victoria and Albert Museum, London. Photograph by Sally Chappell.

Part of an English bed curtain made during the second half of the 17th century in England, worked in herringbone stitch, chain stitch, coral stitch, stem stitch, long and short stitch, feather stitch, buttonhole stitch, satin stitch, braid stitch, and knotted chain or link stitch. Given by Mr. G. Baron Ash. Courtesy of Victoria and Albert Museum, London. Photograph by Sally Chappell.

This is part of an English bed curtain made in the late 17th century, worked in stem stitch, chain stitch, back stitch, and knotted chain stitch (not discussed in this book). Courtesy of Victoria and Albert Museum, London. Photograph by Sally Chappell.

Detail of a curtain embroidered in England in 1680. Crown Copyright, Victoria and Albert Museum, London.

A section of the bed hangings and valances made by Abigail Pett during the late 17th century in England. The hangings and valances are embroidered with crewel wools in long and short stitch, stem stitch, satin stitch, split stitch, feather stitch, and herringbone stitch with laid and couch work. Courtesy of Victoria and Albert Museum, London. Photograph by Sally Chappell.

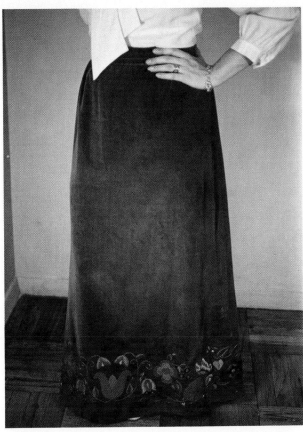

Velveteen skirt designed and embroidered by Ellen Silver in six-strand embroidery cotton thread.

Stylized flowers designed by the author and worked by Ellen Silver in crewel yarn in split stitch, weaving stitch, French knots, stem stitch, coral knot stitch, spider web stitch, fishbone stitch, satin stitch, and double-threaded running stitch.

Detail of the skirt designed and stitched by Ellen Silver in six-strand embroidery cotton.

All photos this section by Anne Tucker

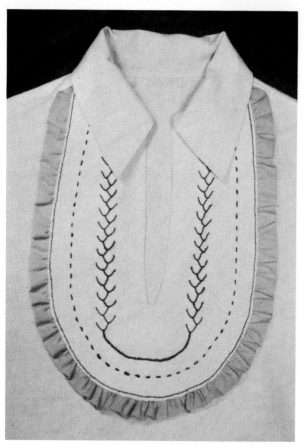

Detail of a shirt; pattern designed and worked by the author in feather and running stitches.

Orange and red flowers designed and worked by the author in chain stitch, stem stitch and fishbone stitch.

"Five Tall Mushrooms," designed by the author and worked by Barbara Morgan in weaving stitch, stem stitch, chain stitch, cloud filling stitch, backstitched chain stitch and French knots.

Sampler designed and worked by the author.

Eyeglasses case designed and worked by the author in fly stitch and French knots.

Wrist pincushion designed and worked by the author in buttonhole stitch and bullion knots.

Pillow designed and worked by the author using straight stitch, stem stitch, satin stitch, whipped stem stitch and French knots.

Shoulder bag designed and worked by the author in chain stitch, coral knot stitch, cloud filling stitch, stem stitch and straight stitch.

Wall hanging designed and worked by the author in stem stitch, couching stitch, chain stitch, and cross stitch.

Picture designed and worked by the author in stem stitch, couching stitch, and satin stitch.

3. Slip the needle from below upward between the stitch at point A and the fabric; do not pass through the fabric to the back of the embroidery. Gently pull the yarn through.

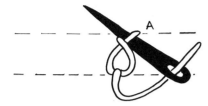

4. Begin the second stitch farther along your upper imaginary line, as pictured. Continue as instructed in steps 1, 2, and 3.

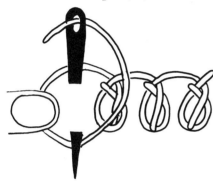

OPEN CHAIN OR ROMAN CHAIN STITCH

This somewhat square version of the chain stitch has open rather than closed links and when stitched, gives the impression of a ladder. Appropriately enough, this stitch was once popularly called the ladder stitch, but it has come to be known as the open chain or the Roman chain stitch. Occasionally used as the casing for ribbon on handmade lingerie, the open chain or Roman chain stitch is more widely used as a border in crewel embroidery pieces. It is most easily worked if you imagine that you are working your stitches along two parallel lines, which are indicated by dotted lines in the illustrations.

1. Bring the needle and the yarn to the surface of the fabric at point A, at the top end of the left parallel line. Pull the yarn through.

Make a loop with the yarn to the right and hold it in place with your left thumb.

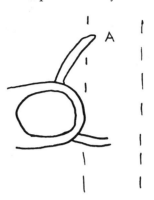

2. Insert the needle at point B, level with point A on the right parallel line. Return the needle to the surface at point C, diagonally across from point B and in line with point A on the left parallel line. Keep the loop of yarn underneath the needle.

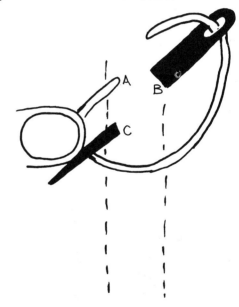

3. Draw the yarn carefully through to the front of the fabric and leave a little slack in the loop. Now make a loop to the right and hold it in place again with your left thumb. Insert the needle at point D, level with point C on the right parallel line, inside the slack first loop. Return the needle to the surface

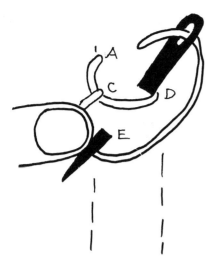

at point E, underneath point C on the left parallel line. The distance between points C and E should be the same as that between points A and C. This distance is one of the factors that determine the size of the stitches. The other size-determining factor is the distance between points A and B and points C and D, and this is why the suggestion has been made of using the two imaginary parallel lines. Pull the yarn through.

4. Continue to the end of the row in the same manner. Tack the last link in place with two small stitches, one on each parallel line

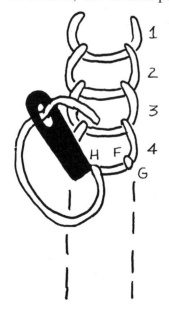

over the last loop, as indicated. If, for instance, you were tacking down stitch No. 4, you should pull the yarn through to the surface of the fabric at point F and insert the needle at point G, close to point F but outside the loop. Pull the yarn to the back of the fabric and return to the surface at point H inside the loop and repeat the tacking stitch.

SINGALESE CHAIN STITCH

A fancy modification of the open chain or Roman chain stitch, the Singalese chain stitch is also used for wide borders. It is essential to master the open chain or Roman chain stitch first, because the Singalese chain stitch is worked in the same manner, but over two strands of a contrasting-colored yarn which are placed along the imaginary parallel lines. The addition of the extra strands of color gives the outer edges of the Singalese chain stitch a candy-cane effect which is quite attractive. If you prefer a bolder stitch, you may work the chain links over four strands of yarn, two along each imaginary line. Do not make the border too wide or the stitch will become unwieldy.

1. For purposes of clarity, I will refer to black and white strands of yarn. In this example, the white yarn will be used for the chain-link stitches which are worked over the strands of black yarn. Bring the strands of black yarn to the front of the fabric at the top of the two imaginary lines and let them fall gently along the lines. Bring the white yarn to the surface of the material at point A, along the left parallel line, slightly below and inside the point where the black yarn emerges.(See page 35, top left.)

2. Make a loop to the right and hold it in place with your left thumb. Pass the needle and yarn from left to right under both black

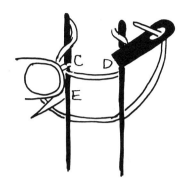

strands and insert the needle at point B, which is on the right parallel, directly opposite point A and inside the black strand of yarn. Bring the needle to the surface at point C, on the left parallel line, diagonally opposite point B, keeping the loop and the black strand of yarn underneath the needle.

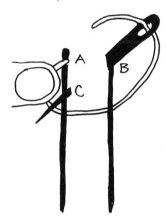

Draw the yarn through to the surface of the fabric. Leave some slack in the loop; do not pull the yarn too tight or you will distort the stitch.

3. Begin the second stitch by making a loop to the right. Hold the loop in place with your left thumb. Slip the needle and yarn (from left to right) underneath both strands of black yarn and insert the needle at point D, on the right parallel line, directly opposite point C but inside the black strand and the previous link. Bring the needle to the surface of the fabric at point E, on the left parallel line diagonally across from point D, keeping the strand of black yarn and the loop under-

neath the needle point. Pull the yarn to the surface of the fabric, again being certain you do not pull the yarn too tight and you leave the loop slightly slack.

4. Continue in this manner to the end of the row. To secure the last stitch in the row, tack down the final link as instructed in step 4 of the section about the open chain or Roman chain stitch (page 34). Then thread one strand of the black yarn into an embroidery needle and insert the needle slightly below the last link, but along the imaginary

line. Pull the yarn through to the back side of the embroidery and end off in the normal fashion. Repeat this with the second strand of black yarn. If the black strands become tangled while you are stitching the chain links, a firm pull on the black strand after it has been brought to the back side of the material will straighten the yarn.

DETACHED CHAIN OR LAZY DAISY STITCH

These chain stitches are not joined together as in the other varieties of chain stitch but are separate links individually anchored by a small stitch taken at the base of the loop. Excellent for flower petals, the detached chain stitch may also be worked as a filler, either sprinkled at random or set in ordered rows. You may be interested in trying this stitch as a border by working each chain in an alternate direction—one right side up, one upside down, one right side up. Any number of strands of yarn may be used to work this versatile stitch.

1. Draw the needle and yarn to the front of the material at point A. (In this case we shall make the first petal of an imaginary flower, the outline of which is pictured in the diagram. Form a loop in the direction of the outline that you are covering. Hold it down with either your left or right thumb—whichever is more convenient for you.

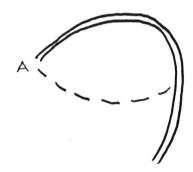

2. Insert the needle at point A again and come up at point B, in a line with point A and inside the yarn loop. Carefully draw the yarn through to the front of the fabric to form the first stitch. Do not pull the yarn tight, or the stitch will be destroyed.

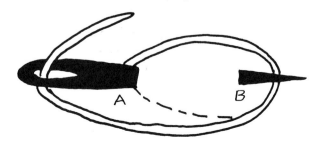

3. Anchor the stitch at the bottom of the link by taking a small stitch over the loop to point C, very close to point B. See the finished effect in the illustration.

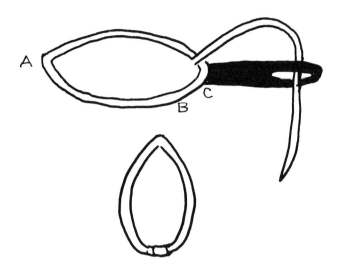

THREADED CHAIN STITCH

Best suited for lines and borders, the threaded chain stitch is actually a row of evenly spaced detached chain (also called the lazy daisy chain) stitches (see the previous section which explains the formation of this stitch) threaded with complementary, contrasting, or the same-colored yarn. Similar to working the threaded back stitch and the double threaded running stitch, this stitch may be threaded either in one direction, yielding a graceful line joining the detached chain (lazy daisy chain) stitches, or in two directions, giving the pleasing impression of alternating large and small circles of different colors or of the same color. A tapestry needle should be used when the threading step commences. Any number of strands of yarn may be used with this decorative stitch as long as a balance is maintained between the threading and the foundation stitches. Although it is by no means mandatory, you may find it easier to work this stitch in a frame in the beginning to ensure that the threading is even.

1. Stitch a row of evenly spaced detached chain (lazy daisy) stitches as shown.

2. Bring the needle to the front of the fabric at point A, inside the first link, as shown. Pull the yarn through. Rethread the yarn into a tapestry needle.

3. Place the needle perpendicular to stitch 2 and slip it between the stitch and the fabric as shown. Gently pull the needle and yarn toward you until the yarn forms a soft semi-circle between stitches 1 and 2.

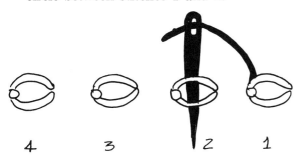

4. Turn the needle upside down and slip it between the fabric and stitch 3 as shown. Again gently pull the yarn through, this time away from you, until there is a semi-circle of yarn between stitches 2 and 3. Continue in this manner until the end of the row.

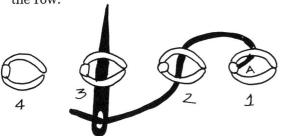

5. At the end of the row, remove the tapestry needle and rethread the yarn into an embroidery needle. Pierce the fabric at point B as shown and carefully pull the yarn to the back side of the fabric. End off in the normal fashion.

6. To thread the stitch a second time, bring the needle up at point C, inside stitch 4, as shown. Rethread the yarn into a tapestry needle and repeat steps 3 and 4.

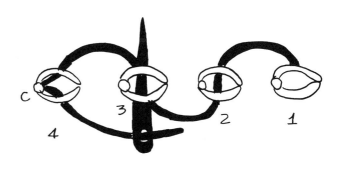

TÊTE-DE-BOEUF STITCH
(Bull's Head Stitch)

This stitch quite obviously gets its name from its shape, for indeed, the tête-de-boeuf stitch does resemble a bull's head. It is a combination of two stitches, the detached chain or lazy daisy stitch (see the section on page 36 which discusses this stitch in detail) and the fly stitch (which is mentioned on page 42). The tête-de-boeuf stitch is a useful and distinctive filling stitch, especially when placed in alternating rows. It can also be used as a border stitch when the stitches are placed one next to the other. There are no restrictions as to the number of strands of yarn that can be used with this stitch.

1. To begin, make the basic fly stitch (page 42). Bring the needle to the surface at point A and pull the yarn through. Make a loop to the right and insert the needle at point B. Return the needle to the surface at point C, which is slightly below and midway between points A and B. Keep the yarn loop underneath the needle. Pull the yarn through.

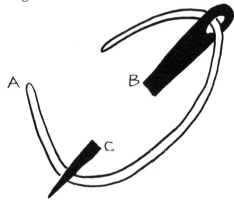

2. Next, make the detached chain or lazy daisy stitch. Make a loop to the right and hold it in place with your left thumb. Insert the needle again at point C and bring the needle to the surface at point D inside the loop. Pull the yarn through.

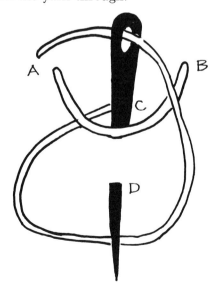

3. Tack the stitch at the bottom by making a small stitch over the loop as close to point D as possible.

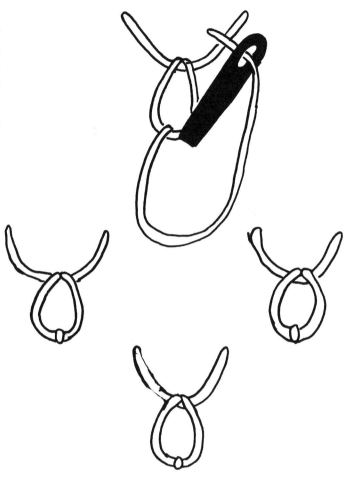

ZIGZAG CHAIN STITCH

Another variation of the chain stitch, the zigzag chain, is actually the chain stitch worked at opposing angles rather than in a line. A whimsical border stitch, the zigzag chain is most attractively displayed if it is worked set apart from other stitches. As in the chain stitch, the heaviness of this stitch varies with an increase in the number of strands of yarn used to embroider it. Again be careful not to use too many strands of yarn with too small a stitch, or the finished effect will not be clear-cut.

1. Bring the needle and the yarn to the front of the material at point A. Form a loop to the right. Hold the loop down with your left thumb, as you did when you embroidered the chain stitch.

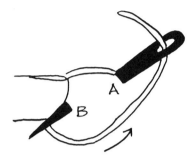

2. Insert the needle again at point A and come out at point B, with the needle point on top of the yarn loop. Point B is to the left and at an angle to point A rather than directly on a line with point A, as in the simple chain stitch. The degree of the angle is entirely up to you, but the angle should be wide enough to be noticeable. Gently pull the yarn through to the front of the material to form the first link. As you did in sewing the chain stitch, temper and control the tightness of the yarn as you draw it to the surface. Allow the yarn to lie naturally against the fabric.

3. Insert the needle at point B, now inside the first stitch, and form a loop to the right. Hold the loop down with your left thumb. Come to the surface of the fabric at point C, to the right of point B and at approximately the same angle to point B as point B is to point A in step 2. The direction of the angle of the stitches alternates from left to right. That is to say, if the first stitch zigs to the left, then the second stitch should zag to the right.

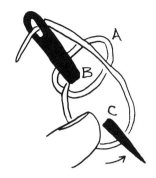

4. Continue zigging and zagging the links to the end of the row. Anchor the last link with a small straight stitch.

The Loop Stitches

BUTTONHOLE STITCHES

Formed by catching a loop of yarn underneath the needle, the buttonhole stitch (which is also referred to as the blanket stitch) is a multifaceted stitch. It may be sewn close together or far apart, in a circle or in rows, as a border with two varying lengths of stitches or back to back. It follows sloping curves or straight lines. The stitch is equally pleasing when worked with one, two, or three strands of yarn.

1. Bring the needle to the front of the fabric at point A. Pull the yarn through.

2. Form a loop in the direction you are working. This stitch must be worked from the left to the right or from the top to the bottom, as pictured in the accompanying illustrations. Therefore, if you are working the stitch lengthwise, make a loop toward the bottom of the material and to the right; if you are working the stitch across your piece, make the loop toward the right edge of the material. In either case you must keep the loop underneath the point of the needle. Insert the needle at point B, a short distance away from point A at the desired height of the stitch. Come up at point C, slightly inside the line you are covering, with the point of the needle inside the loop. Pull the yarn through the loop.

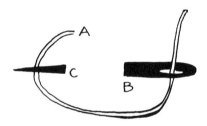

3. Make another loop downward and to the right. Insert the needle at point D, the desired distance away from but still on a line with point B. Come up at point E, even with point C and parallel to point D, again with the loop underneath the needle point. Pull through and slightly inside the line you are covering.

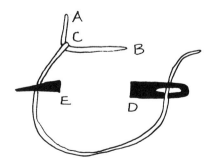

4. Continue in the same manner, repeating step 2 to the end of the row. Tack the final buttonhole stitch with a tiny stitch over the last loop. The final illustration shows closely worked buttonhole stitches.

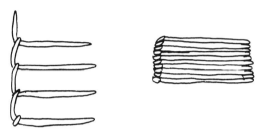

DOUBLE BUTTONHOLE STITCH

An attractive border, the double buttonhole stitch is merely two rows of buttonhole stitches facing each other. Working the stitch in two colors adds an interesting highlight to this border. There is no rule as to the number of strands of yarn.

1. Work a row of buttonhole stitches from left to right or from top to bottom of your piece. Anchor the final stitch.

2. Turn your piece upside down and work another row of buttonhole stitches, either from right to left or bottom to top of your fabric. The arms of the second row of stitches should be centered between the arms of the first row of stitches. Anchor the second row of stitches. See the accompanying illustration for the finished stitches.

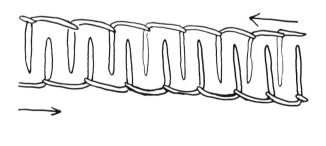

STEM STITCH

This exceedingly flexible stitch adheres to the line of any curve. Worked in rows, the stem stitch is a close filler, and worked separately, it is a useful line stitch. Always work the stitch in the same direction when filling a space.

As a general rule the loop may be made to either side of the needle with essentially the same effective result. However, once you have chosen the side, you cannot change it in the middle of the row without altering the look of the stitch. To outline a shape with the stem stitch, hold the yarn on the side of the needle away from the shape you are outlining in order to assure a smooth, upright line. One or more strands of yarn may be used to define the boldness of the stitch. One final hint: decrease the size of the stitches as you work around a curve. Otherwise the curve will not be smooth.

1. Draw the needle and the yarn to the front of your piece at point A. Insert the needle at point B. This will establish the size of the first stitch. Holding the yarn to the left side of the needle (in this example) with your left thumb, return the needle to the front of the fabric at point C, half the distance between points A and B.

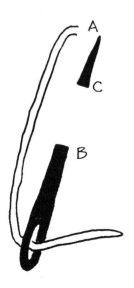

2. Draw the yarn entirely through to the front side of the piece. The anchored end of the yarn will now jut to the right side of the stitch. With your left hand, pull the yarn to the left of the stitch and loop it toward the right. Hold the loop down with your left thumb and insert the needle at point D. (The

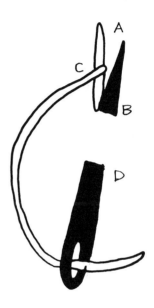

distance BD should be the same distance as BC.) Come up at point B and pull the yarn to the same side of the needle, always completing the stitch on the front of the fabric. To finish the last stitch in the row, simply end it with the yarn and needle on the wrong side of the material, rather than drawing the needle and yarn through to the front of the fabric to form the next stitch.

WHIPPED STEM STITCH

This stitch has the versatility of the stem stitch when it is used as a line stitch, with the additional attraction of a colorful whipping. (The stitch may, of course, be whipped in the same color.) To my eye the most dramatic whipping is done with a contrasting color and with one strand of yarn. Two strands of yarn can often obscure the foundation stitches. The basic stem stitch should be worked with two strands of yarn. Do not make these stitches too large or too small, because this will modify the spacing and the effect of the whipping.

1. Work a row of simple stem stitches, as explained previously.

2. Thread the needle with a yarn of the chosen color. Bring it to the front of the piece slightly below and to the left of the tip of the top stitch. Rethread the yarn into a tapestry needle, and slide the needle between the fabric and the foundation stitch at the juncture of the first two stem stitches, with the needle pointing from the right to the left.

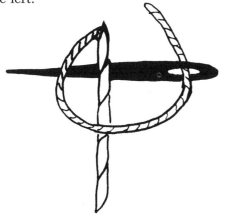

3. Continue to slide the needle between the stitches and the fabric, making certain that the whipping yarn is always coming from the left of the foundation stitches at the completion of each step. The illustration shows the finished whipping.

FLY STITCH

Depending upon the length of the tacking stitch, the fly stitch resembles either a V or a wishbone with an extended joint. Because of their unique shape, fly stitches form a very different border no matter what position they are placed in—upside down, back to back, or face to face. The fly stitch is also quite useful as an open filling stitch if it is scattered within a space or worked in a line. Whatever number of strands of yarn you use, I think you will be pleased with the results.

1. Bring the needle to the front of the fabric at point A. Pull the yarn through. Form a loop to the right and insert the needle at point B, across from and still slightly to the right of point A. This will establish the width of the stitch.
2. Bring the needle to the front side of the fabric at point C, slightly below and yet between points A and B. Keep the yarn loop

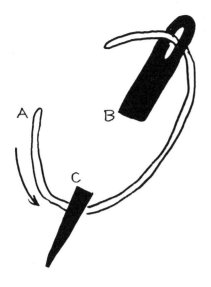

underneath the needle point. Pull the yarn through to the front side of the fabric. As with all the loop stitches, draw the yarn gently and carefully or the stitch will be lost.

3. Tack the stitch with a straight stitch made over loop AB. The length of the anchoring stitch can be long or very short and close to point C, as shown below.

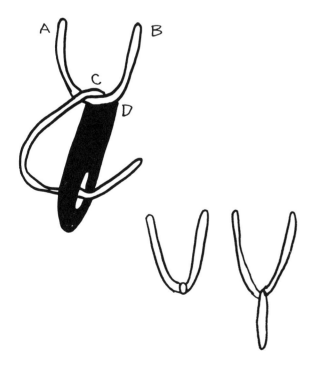

CROWNED FLY STITCH

This relative of the fly stitch is as versatile as its cousin. It, too, may be worked either as a distinctive border or an open filler. The two extra tacking stitches provide an opportunity to vary the look of the stitch. The center stitch can be long and the two side ones short, or all three may be the same length. The width of the stitch may also be changed to coincide with the tacking stitches. Just as in the fly stitch, the crowned fly stitch may be worked with any number of yarn strands.

1. Make a simple fly stitch, as explained in steps 1, 2, and 3 in the section concerning the fly stitch.

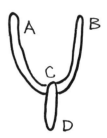

2. Having completed tacking stitch CD, bring the needle to the front of the fabric at point E, slightly to the right of point C. Complete the anchoring by inserting the needle at point F.

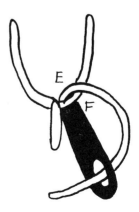

3. Bring the needle to the front side of the fabric again at point G, slightly to the left of point C. Complete this tacking stitch by inserting the needle at point H.

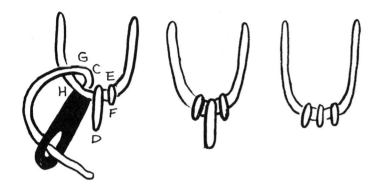

CRETAN STITCH

With the Cretan stitch you will obtain very different effects, depending upon whether the stitches are slanted and close together or well spaced and flat. Because of this quality, the stitch is an especially worthwhile experiment in spacing. Try using it as a border, a lacy tree, or a leaf, both open and solidly worked, and compare the difference. The stitch adapts well to any width. Of course the stitches must not be too long or the embroidery may pull out while it is in use. Any number of strands of yarn are used attractively with this stitch.

1. Draw the needle and the yarn to the front side of the fabric at point A—in this case the tip of the space that we will fill solidly with the Cretan stitch. Make a loop as usual, counterclockwise. Insert the needle at point B, slightly below and to the right of point A. Point B should be close enough to point A so that ultimately no fabric shows between the stitches. Bring the needle to the front of the fabric at point C, needle on top of the loop. Gently pull the yarn through to the

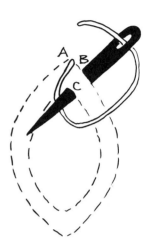

front side of the material, at all times keeping the loop underneath the yarn you are pulling through.

2. Make a loop clockwise this time, and insert the needle at point D, slightly below and to the left of point A. Bring the needle to the front of the fabric at point E, inside and on top of the loop. Point E is slightly below point C on the left side of the shape. Pull the whole length of the yarn to the front side of the fabric, always keeping the loop underneath the yarn strand you are pulling.

3. Continue in this manner to make the stitches, one to the right and one to the left of the center of the shape you are filling. See the finished effect in this illustration.

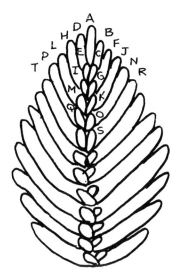

4. If you would like to embroider the Cretan stitch as in the illustration below, increase the distance and flatten the angle between points A and B, as explained in step 1. Similarly, increase the distance and widen the angle between points A and D, as explained in step 2. You should also increase the spacing between points C and E and work the corresponding points G, K, O, and S below point C, and points I, M, and Q below point E. The interest of the stitch is heightened if the stitch becomes increasingly flatter and larger as it progresses away from point A.

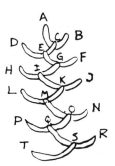

FEATHER STITCH

Equally attractive as a line, border, or band stitch, the feather stitch is easily mastered if, as you work, you picture four parallel lines extending from points A, B, C, and D, as shown on page 46. If you continue with this picture in your mind and work alternating stitches underneath and still parallel with stitches AB and CD, you should achieve a well-spaced stitch without worry. Any number of strands of yarn may be used with the feather stitch.

1. Draw the needle and the yarn to the front of the material at point A. Make a loop counterclockwise. Insert the needle at point B, slightly to the right but in line with point A. The points of all the stitches that follow and are made to the right side should be on a line with points A and B. Come to the surface of the fabric at point C, below but midway between points A and B. The point of the needle should be on top of the yarn loop. Pull the needle and yarn through the loop.

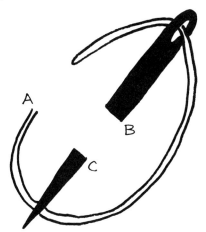

2. Make a loop of yarn clockwise. Insert the needle at point D, slightly to the left but in line with point C. The distance between points C and D should be equal to that be-

tween points A and B. Points C and D are the beginning of the final two parallel lines under which the remaining stitches made on the left-hand side should fall. Come to the front of the fabric at point E, on a line with point A and slightly below points C and D. You will find that point E is also in the center of stitch CD. Pull the yarn through, keeping the loop underneath the yarn.

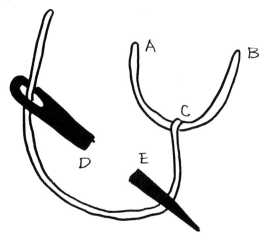

3. The third stitch, EF, is made to the right side. Point F is in line with point B. The center point, G, is in line with point C. Anchor the last loop in the center with a small straight stitch.

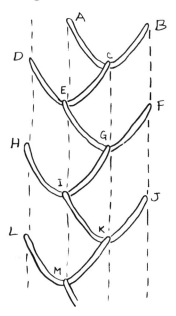

The Knotted Stitches

FRENCH KNOT

One of the oldest embroidery stitches, the French knot is also one of the most flexible stitches. It is a close filling stitch in relief when placed in large or small clusters and in orderly rows. The knots may also be scattered to fill a space lightly. Marvelous for sprinkling in the center of petals of a flower, French knots may also be strategically placed in the curve of a graceful border or outline. The knot, made with either one, two, or three strands of yarn, offers an excellent opportunity to mix colors and shades of colors. The neatest French knots are formed by winding the yarn around the needle only once. Any inclination you may have to enlarge the size will be satisfied better by increasing the number of strands of yarn used to make the knot rather than by increasing the number of times the yarn is wound around the needle.

1. Draw the needle and the yarn to the front of the fabric at point A. Form a loop as shown and hold it down with your left thumb, as pictured in the illustration.

2. Insert the needle in this loop and twist the yarn around the needle once.

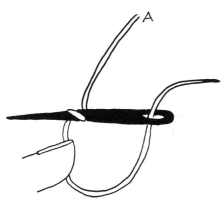

3. Holding the yarn snugly but not tightly around the needle, insert the needle into the fabric at point B, next to point A.

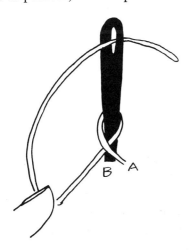

4. Gently draw the needle to the back side of the fabric, completing the first knot. The finished knot is shown below, to the right.
5. Repeat steps 1, 2, 3, and 4 for additional French knots.

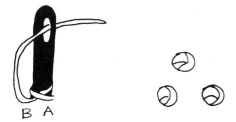

BULLION KNOT

Another knotted stitch, the bullion knot also gives a special texture to embroidery. These long knotted stitches may be worked in clusters, next to one another, or individually. They are lovely flower centers, borders, or additions to borders (similar to the French knot). Best worked with two strands of yarn, the bullion knot also offers a chance to mix colors.

1. Bring the needle to the surface of the fabric at point A and pull the yarn through. Insert the needle at point B, as shown below. This will establish the size of the knot. Return the needle to the surface of the fabric again at point A. Do not pull the yarn or the needle through.

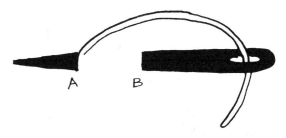

2. Wrap the yarn around the point of the needle from five to nine times. The number of twists depends upon the size of stitch AB. Wrap the yarn around the needle enough times to fill the stitch taken between points A and B.

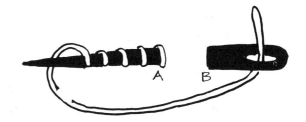

3. Pinch the twists of yarn between your left thumb and index finger. At the same time push the needle through the twists with

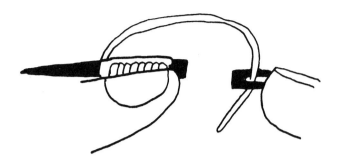

your right index finger. When the needle has moved and the point protrudes enough from the twists so that it can be grasped, carefully draw the needle and the yarn all the way to the left through the twists. Do not allow the twists to unwind. Be certain that each twist is smooth.

4. Again insert the needle at point B, and pull the yarn through to the back of the fabric. Continue to gently pull the yarn until all the twists fit snugly together. The finished knot is shown below, at the right.

A   B

CORAL STITCH

A decorative line stitch, the coral stitch is a series of equally spaced knots in a line. The spacing of the knots can be close together or far apart, depending upon the effect desired. The more frequent the knots, the more nubbed the over-all finish. When the stitch is worked in several rows close together, it becomes a good, solid filler. If you do use this stitch as a close filler, you must alternate the placement of the knots in each row to ensure that no fabric shows

through your stitching. Properly executed, solid rows of the coral stitch resemble rows of French knots. As a line stitch the coral stitch follows curves very well. It is advisable to work this stitch with at least two strands of yarn to attain maximum effectiveness.

1. Draw the needle and the yarn to the surface of the material at point A. Lay the yarn against fabric in the direction in which you are stitching. Make a loop to the right and hold the loop in place with your left thumb.

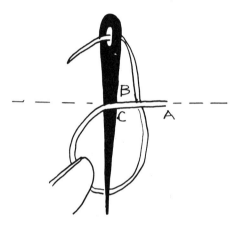

2. Take a small stitch at points B and C, slightly to the left of point A and perpendicular to the line to be covered. As you return the needle to the front of the fabric at point C, place the loop underneath the point. The distance between point A and the stitch BC determines the distance between knots. This spacing should remain consistent.

3. Draw the needle through the loop until the knot is formed. Repeat the previous steps to produce the finished effect as pictured in the illustration.

ZIGZAG CORAL STITCH

As the name implies, the zigzag coral stitch is simply the coral stitch worked in a zigzag line. This stitch is used as a border stitch, whose width is controlled by the spacing of the knots. Two or three evenly spaced rows of zigzag coral stitches make an especially interesting and somewhat textured border when a simple edging is needed. The stitch is most attractively worked with two or more strands of yarn. The easiest way to ensure that the border is as wide as you desire and straight is to imagine that you are working along two parallel lines.

1. Bring the needle to the front of the fabric at point A at the beginning of the top parallel line (as indicated by the dotted lines in the drawing) and pull the yarn through. Lay the yarn along the line in the direction in which you are working. Hold the yarn in place with your left thumb and put the needle perpendicular to the line. Take a small stitch at point B and come out at point C, as indicated.

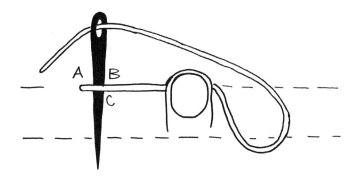

2. Make a loop over your thumb and underneath the needle as indicated. Pull the yarn and needle through to complete stitch BC until the loop begins to tighten around your left thumb. Remove your thumb and continue to pull the yarn gently until the knot is tight.

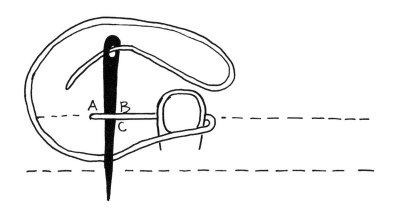

3. To make the second stitch, put the needle perpendicular to the bottom line diagonally across from stitch BC and hold the yarn along the line and near the spot where you plan to make stitch DE. Take a small stitch

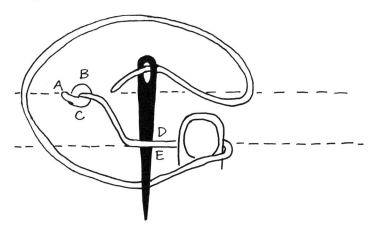

DE as indicated and again make a loop over your thumb and underneath the needle. Pull the yarn through until it begins to tighten around your thumb. Remove your thumb and pull the yarn gently until the knot is tight. Continue in this manner until the row is completed. If you find that you must work this stitch from right to left, the stitch is made the same way with the exception that

the loop over your thumb will be made from the left to the right, rather than, as in this example, from the right to the left.

Note: This is an alternative method of working the coral stitch. Do experiment with both techniques and choose the one you find easier.

Cross-stitched towel (detail). Courtesy of the Brooklyn Museum

The Cross Stitches

CROSS STITCH

One of the very basic and most widely used embroidery stitches, the cross stitch is well placed in any design. Small or large, this stitch is attractive as a border, a line, or an open filler. Whole designs may be beautifully worked entirely in this stitch. One of the important things to remember when you embroider the cross stitch in a line is that every stitch must touch the next at all four points. Distinctness of each individual stitch is also imperative here. Carefully stabbing the needle through the material and working the stitch with the fabric in a frame will help to give your stitches this quality. Any number of strands of yarn may be used with the cross stitch.

1. Bring the needle and the yarn to the front of the fabric at point A. Point A will be at the bottom left leg of the first cross stitch. Insert the needle at point B, diagonally to point A. This establishes the height of your stitch. Pull the yarn to the back of the fabric. Return the needle to the surface of the piece at point C, directly below B and in line with point A. Draw the yarn to the front of the fabric.

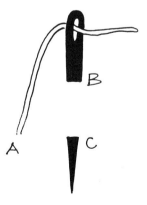

2. Insert the needle at point D, diagonally to point C and in line with point B. This is half of the second cross stitch. Pull the yarn through to the back of the fabric. Bring the needle and the yarn to the front of the material at point E, directly below point D and in line with points A and C. Pull the yarn to the front of the fabric. Continue to the end of the row, making one diagonal of each stitch.

the needle exactly at point D. Continue in this fashion to the end of the row. Illustration shows the finished effect.

4. To work the cross stitch as an open filling stitch, draw the needle and the yarn to the front of the fabric at point A, as pictured in

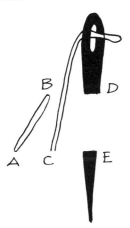

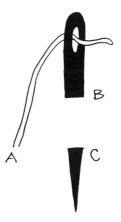

3. Having completed the first half of the stitches, you will now work in the opposite direction to finish the second leg of the stitches. Bring the needle to the front of the fabric at point I and insert it again exactly at point F, crossing over stitch GH. Pull the yarn through. Come to the surface again at point G, cross over stitch EF and insert

the illustration. Insert the needle at point B, diagonally to point A. Pull the yarn through to the back of the material. Come to the front of the fabric at point C, in line with point B. Pull the yarn through. This is the first diagonal of the stitch.

5. Insert the needle at point D, diagonally to point C and on a line with point B. Pull the

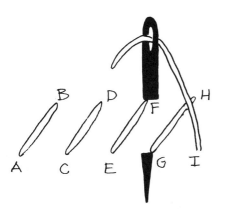

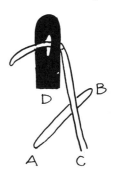

yarn through. This completes the stitch. To begin another separate cross stitch, bring the needle to the front of the fabric at point A of the second stitch. An example of the cross stitch used as an open filler is pictured in this illustration.

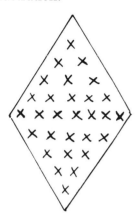

BRICK AND CROSS FILLING STITCH

The brick and cross filling stitch was used quite often in Jacobean embroidery (mentioned in the chapter about the history of crewel embroidery). Although it is a combination of two basic embroidery stitches, the cross stitch and the straight stitch, the effect is quite special when it is worked into a design. The cross stitch is placed between two groups of horizontal or vertical straight stitches which are placed in checkerboard rows. Because this is such a distinctive filling stitch, I do caution you to be selective when you place the stitch in a design, so that it does not unbalance your piece.

1. Begin by making four horizontal straight stitches one next to the other as shown. (The straight stitch is discussed in a previous section in this book.) The straight stitches should be as long as the width of one cross stitch.

2. Work a single cross stitch as instructed in the section about this stitch (page 51).

3. Work four more horizontal straight stitches and another single cross stitch. Continue in this manner to the end of the row.

4. To begin the second row, work a single cross stitch below the four straight stitches and four straight stitches below the cross stitch in the first row. Proceed with the pattern, working straight stitches below cross stitches and cross stitches below straight stitches to the end of the second row. Work the third row in the same pattern as the first row, and the fourth row in the same pattern as the second. See the finished effect in the illustration.

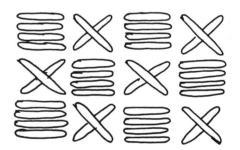

HERRINGBONE STITCH

A wide diagonal crossing of two stitches, the herringbone stitch may be worked as an open filling stitch as well as a border and line stitch. The height of the stitch can vary according to your taste (obviously the height should be uniform in stitches that are related), but consistent, even spacing must be maintained or the effect of the stitch will be lost. Keeping the stitches evenly spaced may be difficult in the beginning, but the practice required to master this stitch is well worth the effort. The number of strands of yarn used may be varied according to your objective.

1. Bring the needle and the yarn to the front of the piece at point A. Insert the needle at point B, diagonally across from point A. (This stitch determines the height of the remaining stitches.) Bring the needle to the front at point C, a short distance to the left of and on a line with point B. Draw the yarn to the front of the fabric. This establishes the beginning of the second stitch.

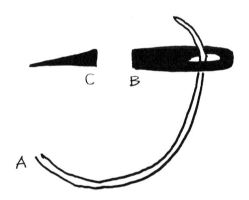

2. Insert the needle at point D, to the right of and on a line with point A. Bring the needle to the front at point E, to the left of and on a line with point D and directly below point B. Pull the yarn through.

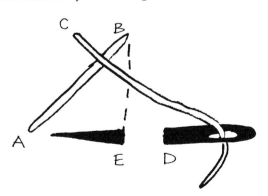

3. Insert the needle at point F, diagonally to point E and in line with points C and B. Bring the needle to the front again at point G, to the left of and in line with point F and directly above point D, as indicated by the dotted line in the illustration. Pull the yarn to the front.

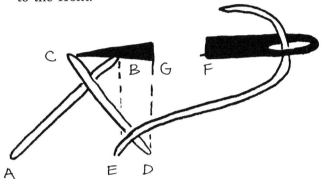

4. Insert the needle at point H, diagonally to point G and in line with points A, E, and D. Come to the surface at point I, a short distance to the left of and in line with point H and directly below point F. Continue in this pattern to the completion of the row. A finished row is pictured in the illustration.

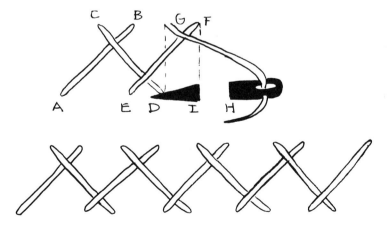

THREADED HERRINGBONE STITCH

A decorative version of the herringbone stitch, the threaded herringbone stitch, makes an attractive border or line. Working the foundation stitches and the threading in contrasting colors enhances the beauty of this stitch. The foundation stitches should not be too small, because this will reduce the impact of the stitch. Use a single strand of yarn to thread the foundation stitches. Make the foundation stitches with two strands of yarn.

1. Work a row of herringbone stitches as explained previously.

2. Begin the threading at the top of the stitch farthest to the right. Bring the needle to the surface at point A, next to and outside the leg of this stitch. Pull the yarn through. Rethread a tapestry needle with the yarn. Point the needle to the right and slide it between the leg of the stitch and the fabric. Pull the yarn gently.

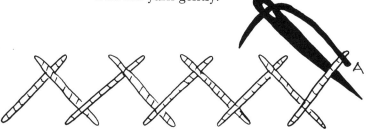

3. With the needle pointing to the top of your fabric, slide it between the material and the second leg of the first stitch. Let the yarn fall gently across the crossing of the two diagonal legs as you pull it through.

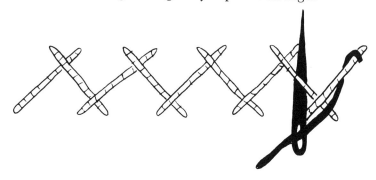

4. With the needle pointing toward the bottom of the piece, slide it between the fabric and the first leg of the second stitch. Again let the yarn fall naturally into place across the juncture of the two stitches. Repeat step 2, then 3, then 2—alternating these two steps to the end of the row.

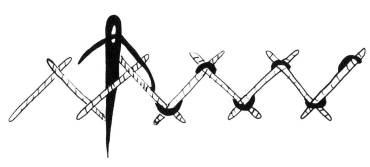

TIED HERRINGBONE STITCH

Another embellishment of the herringbone stitch is the tied herringbone stitch, in which the coral stitch is tied over the crossing of the foundation stitches. Most attractive as a wide border stitch, the tied herringbone stitch is best worked with two strands of yarn for both the foundation stitches and the knots. Of course, the more strands of yarn used to work the tied herringbone stitch, the more of a relief stitch it becomes. The coral stitch is usually worked in a yarn of a contrasting color to display the entire stitch in its most advantageous form.

1. Work a row of herringbone stitches as outlined in the section about this stitch on pages 52-53.

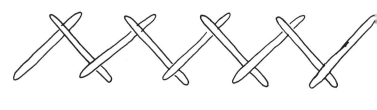

2. Bring the needle to the surface of the fabric underneath the cross of the first herringbone stitch. Pull the yarn to the surface. Slide the needle vertically through the crossing of the first two stitches.

3. Wrap the yarn around the needle as pictured and pull the yarn tight. Work the knot over every crossing in the row, always being certain that the needle is facing toward the center of the herringbone stitch that is being knotted. At no time during the knotting step does the needle pass through the fabric.

4. To secure the contrasting yarn when the row is completed, pass the needle through the material underneath the last crossing after it is knotted, and end off in the normal manner.

FISHBONE STITCH

The fishbone stitch can be worked tightly or openly in a space, producing two different effects. Tiny fishbone stitches also make a dainty border. One of the most popular and attractive uses of the fishbone stitch is in embroidering leaves. The stitch is more effective if an even edge is maintained, so a bit of practicing may be required. Because the spokes of the stitch overlap one another slightly, no more than two, or at the most three, strands of yarn should be used, or the crossing may become bulky.

1. Make a straight stitch, AB, at the peak of the shape that you are filling. Return the needle to the front side of the fabric at point C, to the left of and close to point A along the outline of the shape.

2. Imagine that there are two parallel lines ⅛ to ¼ inch apart down the center of your shape, as drawn in the illustrations. Insert

the needle at point D along the right imaginary line, diagonally to point C. Bring the needle to the front side of the piece at point E, close to but not touching point A.

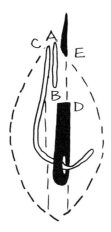

3. Insert the needle at point F along the left imaginary line, diagonally to point E, forming stitch EF.

4. Continue making close diagonal stitches along the imaginary lines down the center

of your shape. It may be easier to practice the stitch if you lightly pencil in these guidelines. Remember that they will show through the stitches if you are working an open fishbone, so be sparing with the pencil marks. Although marking with a pencil is not a good habit to develop, I feel it is a suggestion worth mentioning to the beginner, to be used only when practicing.

VANDYKE STITCH

Most easily worked with the fabric in a frame, the Vandyke stitch can be adapted as an attractive filler, line, or border which has the look of a braid. This stitch can also become an especially effective band stitch when worked either singly or in numerous rows. The size, spacing, and uniformity of tension of the stitch govern the dimension of the braid. The closer and smaller the stitch is, the more noticeable the braid is. Maintaining consistent tightness in your stitching does not mean that you should pull the yarn so taut that the material puckers. Just be certain that each stitch is pulled with the same amount of force to assure a smooth braid. This stitch is equally attractive when worked with various numbers of strands of yarn.

1. Draw the needle and the yarn to the front of the material at point A. Insert the needle at point B, diagonally to point A. Pull the yarn to the back of the piece. Return the needle to the front of the fabric at point C. Pull the yarn through.

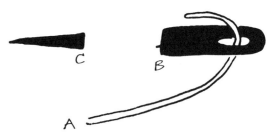

2. Insert the needle at point D, diagonally to point C and on a line with point A. Bring the needle out again to the surface at point E, diagonally below point D and even with point A. Pull the yarn through. You will have formed a cross stitch.

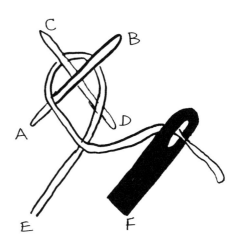

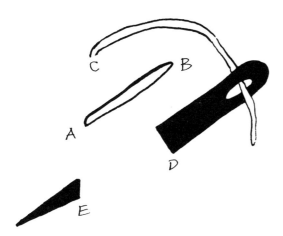

4. Bring the needle to the surface at point G and repeat step 3. Continue in the same manner to the end of the row.

3. With the needle point facing the left, slide the needle between stitch ABCD and the surface of the material. Pull the yarn

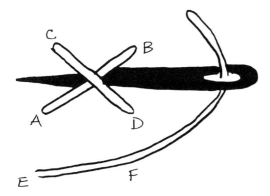

through. Then insert the needle at point F, in line with point E and directly below point D. Gently pull the yarn to the back of the fabric.

5. To work this stitch close together, increase the angle at the crossing of stitches AB and CD. This is accomplished by making the distance between points B and C smaller in step 1. Point E in step 2 should then be closer to point A than it is pictured in the illustration. As a matter of fact, points E and F can be touching points A and D, if that amount of closeness is desired. The length of the stitches may be successfully increased or decreased to conform to a shape without any damage to the look of the stitch. In fact, this is part of the versatility of this stitch.

UPRIGHT CROSS STITCH

The upright cross stitch is a perpendicular crossing of two stitches. When worked in rows this stitch may be used as an open filling stitch or in a wide band. In this case both legs of the stitch should touch the surrounding stitches. As with the cross stitch, it is important that each individual stitch be clear-cut. Securing the fabric in a frame and stabbing the needle distinctly will help you to sew clear stitches. This will also aid in maintaining an equality of size in your stitching. The upright cross stitch may be large or small, but the stitches worked in one area of your design should, of course, be the same size. The number of strands of yarn used to embroider this stitch may be varied.

1. Work a row of back stitches as explained on pages 17-18.

2. Bring the needle and the yarn to the front of the fabric at point A, above and in the center of the first back stitch. Insert the needle at point B, in line with point A and below the first back stitch. Point B should be the same distance from the back stitch as point A. Pull the yarn through.

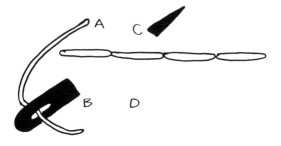

3. Return the needle to the surface at point C, in line with point A and in the center of the second back stitch. Pull the yarn through. Insert the needle at point D, in line with

point B and directly below point C. Pull the yarn to the back of the fabric.

4. Repeat step 3 to the end of the row. See the illustration for the finished stitch.

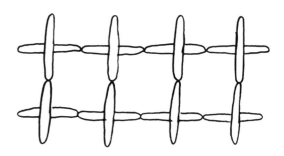

STAR STITCH

A combination of the cross stitch and the upright cross stitch, the star stitch is a very interesting open filler when scattered at random or placed in rows. Because this stitch is worked in three layers—a cross stitch, an upright cross stitch, and another cross stitch—size plays an important role in enhancing the over-all effect. Tiny stitches become a jumble by the third step. Make the foundation cross stitch large enough so that each separate stitch is distinguishable in the finished product. Remember that too many strands of yarn used in combination with small stitches can blur the final effect. Be certain to make a large foundation stitch if you plan to use more than one strand of yarn. As you can readily understand, clarity is especially relevant to the successful execution of the star stitch. Embroidering this stitch will be facilitated by the use of a frame.

1. The foundation cross stitch will be made in this step. Draw the needle to the surface of the material at point A. Insert the needle at point B, diagonally to point A. This diagonal should be flatter than the ones that you formed to make the basic cross stitch. This allows for extra room in which to fit the final

Wall hanging: "Primitive" by Evelyn Svec Ward, worked in deep red, tans, grays, rust, black, and brown using wool and "copper lurex" on natural linen. Done in stem stitch, threaded stem stitch, French knot, cross stitch, and open chain stitch. Courtesy of the artist. Photo by William E. Ward.

cross stitch. Pull the yarn through to the back of the fabric. Return the needle to the front of the fabric at point C, directly below point B and in line with point A. Complete

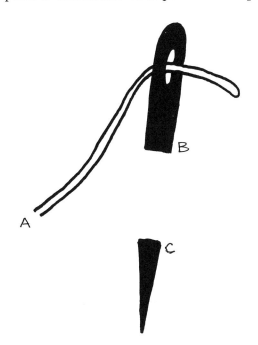

the second diagonal leg of this cross stitch by inserting the needle at point D. Pull the yarn through.

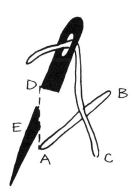

2. Begin to make the upright cross stitch by bringing the needle to the surface at point E, midway along an imaginary line between points A and D. The dotted line in the diagram below is the imaginary line. Insert the needle at point F, in line with point E and now along the imaginary line between

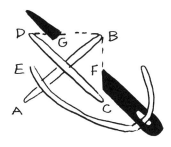

points B and C. Pull the yarn through to the back of the material. Return the needle to the surface at point G, in the center of a third imaginary line, between points B and D.

3. Complete the upright cross stitch by inserting the needle at point H, in the center of a fourth imaginary line, between points A and C. Pull the yarn through.

4. To work the final cross stitch inside the diagonals of the foundation stitch, return the needle to the surface of the fabric at point I, one-quarter of the way up the first diagonal of the foundation stitch and between points A and H. Now make a small cross stitch (IJKL) as shown in the diagram.

The Woven Stitches

WEAVING STITCH

Resembling woven fabric when completed, the weaving stitch gives a charming look to any piece. Especially attractive if worked in two contrasting colors or two different shades of a color, this stitch provides another opportunity to exercise your talents in combining colors. The foundation stitches must be laid with a minimum of two strands of yarn or they will not be pronounced. The weaving may be done with as little as one strand or as many as four. Contrasting the boldness of the foundation stitches with the weaving can produce very interesting effects. Working the foundation stitches with two, three, or four strands of yarn, and the weaving with one strand, for example, gives a much different look to the stitch than if the foundation stitches are worked with three strands of yarn and the weaving is done with the same number of strands. Outlining the weaving stitch is unsuccessful; therefore, keeping the foundation stitches even is imperative. Work this stitch with the fabric held in a frame to assure maximum clarity and consistent tension in your stitching.

1. The first step in working this stitch involves making the foundation stitches that will later be woven. Bring the needle and the yarn to the front of the material at point A. Insert the needle at point B and pull the yarn through. This completes the first stitch. You will see that these foundation stitches

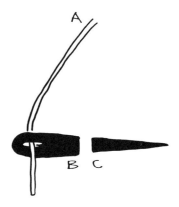

are straight stitches. Return the needle to the surface of the fabric at point C, slightly to the right of point B. The stitch between points B and C should be approximately as wide as the yarn you are using to lay the foundation stitches. Complete the second foundation stitch by inserting the needle at point D, in line with point A. Pull the yarn through. Take a small stitch to the right of point D, the same size as the stitch between points B and C. Come to the surface at point E. Continue in this manner to fill

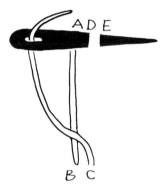

the shape with evenly spaced foundation stitches. These stitches may be shortened or lengthened to conform to the outline of the shape you are filling with the weaving stitch, but they must be evenly spaced.

2. With the second color of yarn begin to weave in the center of your shape, or at the widest part if the width varies. Bring the needle to the surface of the piece at point 1, as pictured in the illustration. Change the embroidery needle for a tapestry needle. Weave the yarn over and under the foundation stitches. Return the needle and the yarn to the back of the fabric at the end of the row at point 2.

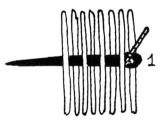

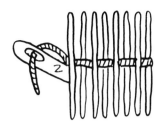

3. Come to the surface again at point 3, one strand of yarn's width above the first row

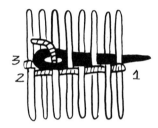

of weaving. Repeat the weaving process, this time going over the strands you passed under, and under the strands you passed over in the first row of weaving. Return the needle to the back of the fabric at the end of the second row of weaving at point 4. Again make a small stitch one strand's width above the second row of weaving and come to the surface at point 5 in the illustration below. Weave the third row in the same fashion as you did the first row.

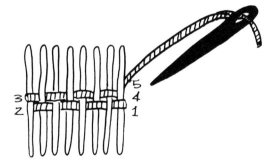

4. Continue to weave over and under the foundation stitches until the top half of the shape is completely filled. Then repeat steps 2 and 3 in the bottom half of the shape.

WOVEN SPIDER WEB STITCH

Another unusually decorative stitch, the woven spider web is worked in a circle. The spokes that originate from the center of the circle are woven either loosely or tightly with a contrasting or same color yarn, depending upon the desired effect. If you work the spokes and the weaving in different colors, the spokes will show through loose weaving. Tightly woven spider webs worked in contrasting colors will obscure the spokes completely, with the exception of the center of the stitch. The weaving may be limited to the center of the stitch and the spokes may be left untouched. In any case, this stitch is complemented by an unelaborate outline, such as the stem stitch. The woven spider web can be worked with five, seven, or nine spokes. There is no specified number as long as there are an odd number of spokes. You may work this stitch with any number of strands of yarn; however, the larger, more tightly woven webs seem to be more effective if woven with one strand of yarn.

1. To make the foundation stitches, bring the needle to the surface of the fabric at point A, in the center of the circle. Make a straight stitch to point B, on the edge of the circle. Draw the yarn through. Return the needle and the yarn to the front of the fabric at point A and make a second straight stitch to point C, slightly to the right of point B. Pull the yarn through to the back of the fabric. Continue to make evenly spaced straight stitches, each time returning to point A in the center of the circle, until you have completed the number of foundation stitches you have planned to sew. Anchor the yarn as usual.

2. Using either the same color of yarn used for the foundation stitches or a contrasting color, bring a new strand of yarn to the front of the piece close to the center of the

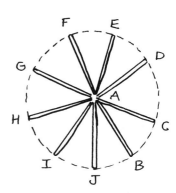

circle between points B and C. Pull the yarn to the surface. Thread the yarn in a tapestry needle. Begin to weave the yarn around the circle. Pass the yarn over spoke B, under spoke J, over spoke I, under spoke H, over spoke G, under spoke F, over spoke E, under spoke D, and over spoke C. Gently pull the

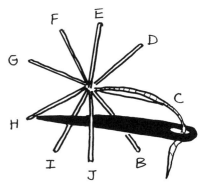

yarn through each time you pass over or under a spoke of the web. Continue to weave over and under each spoke until the web is filled to your specifications. If you find that the strand of yarn is not long enough to complete the weaving, change to an embroidery needle and anchor the yarn in the usual manner underneath the nearest "under" spoke. Bring the new strand to the surface close to your anchoring spot, change to a tapestry needle, and continue weaving. When you have completed the weaving, anchor the yarn by changing to an embroidery needle and using the method described above.

The Couched Stitches

COUCHING

Couching involves laying a number of strands of yarn along a line and tacking it down with tiny stitches taken over the yarn. Because of the unique nature of this stitch, a variety of colors and strands of yarn may be used. The foundation line may be one or many strands of yarn, a solid color or a mixture of two colors. You may introduce further variations by tacking the foundation yarn down with one or two strands, the same color yarn as the foundation line, or a complementary color of yarn. When the entire stitch is worked with a single color, the line produced is an interesting and novel way to implement an outline. Mixing and contrasting colors in this stitch modifies the result to a multicolored line.

This is one of the most versatile stitches, because you can lay the strands of yarn to be couched in any configuration. The tiny couching stitches add to the maximum mobility of the line. As well as being an attractive outlining stitch, couching may be used as a close filling stitch. It may be worked in adjoining rows within circles, triangles, and hexagons, or in any direction you may have in mind. Furthermore, couching may also be scattered within a shape or randomly in a whole design. This is one of the easiest ways to express yourself freely in crewel embroidery. It is essential that you work this stitch with the fabric held tightly within a frame.

1. Bring the needle and the yarn or strands of yarn that you plan to couch to the front of the fabric at the beginning of the line at point A. Lay the yarn naturally along the line. The partially showing dotted line in the illustration indicates the line to be couched.

2. Using another piece of yarn, bring the needle to the surface from the back of the fabric at point B, a short distance along the line. Place the needle over the strands of yarn and insert it again at point B, forming a small stitch on top of the foundation line to hold it in place. Pull the yarn through to the back of the fabric.

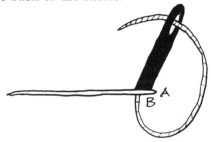

3. Repeat step 2 at short intervals along the strands being couched until you have completed tacking down the yarn. End your stitches off on the back of the fabric.

4. At the end of the row, thread the strands of the foundation line into a needle and insert the needle into the hole of the last couching stitch. Pull the strands through to the back of the material. Clip the ends quite short.

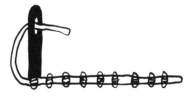

RUMANIAN STITCH

Limited to one color of yarn, the Rumanian stitch is tacked down with a slanting rather than a straight stitch. It is equally distinctive as a close filling stitch or as a broad border stitch. Although the Rumanian stitch is most often worked close together, the stitches may be spaced slightly for a different effect. In order to keep the stitches smooth and to cover the fabric completely, maintain a constant slant with the tacking stitch.

1. Draw the needle and the yarn to the front of the fabric at point A. Insert the needle at point B and return the needle to the surface at point C, slightly to the right of the center of what will be stitch AB. Point C should be the width of the yarn you are using above stitch AB. Pull the yarn through to the front of the fabric to allow stitch AB to lie flat against the material.

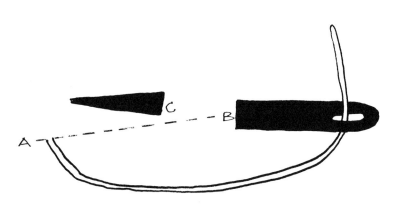

2. Make a small diagonal stitch toward the left over stitch AB at point D. Pull the yarn through to the back of the fabric.

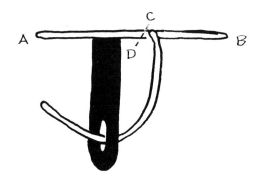

3. Begin the second stitch by returning the needle and yarn to the front of the fabric at point E, close to point A. Insert the needle at point F, close to point B. Leave a loop of yarn and return to the surface at point G, close to and below point C. Pull the yarn to the surface of the fabric with the needle inside the loop. Tack down stitch EF as you did stitch AB in step 2.

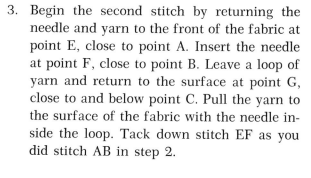

4. Repeat step 3 until you have worked the desired number of stitches. The illustration, below pictures the completed stitches.

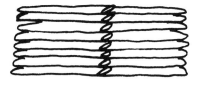

Chapter 3
The Sampler

Now that you have learned the basic stitches of crewel, the next step is putting them to work. One of the most sensible methods of doing this is to make a sampler of stitches. In this way you can practice all—or at least a majority—of the stitches in order to discover which ones you enjoy embroidering (I have found that I have a number of favorites), which appeal to you esthetically, and which need more practice! You will find that some stitches blend well together, while some make a lovely contrast next to one another. This is a chance to educate your eye to judge which stitches must be set apart by themselves to display their full beauty, and which need not. Combining stitches is a very important part of crewelwork and one of the factors that makes it an art as well as a craft.

This sampler may be your first experience with yarn, fabric, needle, and a frame. It will give your fingers the feel of the yarn worked on fabric—so important in crewelwork. You will have the chance to establish a consistent tension in your stitches; too tight a stitch, one of the most common dangers, will cause the fabric to pucker under the strain of the yarn, while stitches that vary in tension yield an uneven finish. I again emphasize the importance of stabbing the needle directly through the material to ensure distinctness in your stitching. You should make each stitch with care, paying special regard to uniformity of size.

I have always encouraged people to experiment with different thicknesses and colors of yarn. In this project I underline the statement. Some stitches vary decidedly in their effect, depending upon the number of strands of yarn or the colors used. For example, French knots become much larger as you increase the number of strands of yarn. The stem stitch is a delicate outline when worked with one strand of yarn, but produces a bolder feeling when worked with two strands. Working a stitch in two shades of a color or two different colors is an area that should not go unexplored either. The whipped and threaded stitches—running, herringbone, and stem, for example—lend themselves quite easily to two colors or two shades of a color. The couching and cloud filling stitches, as well as the double buttonhole stitch, also fall into this category. Well selected colors and thicknesses in your yarn are what give your piece its warmth and textures, so do not cheat yourself by overlooking these two important aspects of crewel as you work your sampler.

There are any number of shapes your sampler can take. Traditionally, it is thought to be a long narrow piece of fabric sewn with various stitches which can be added to at will. In this form, your piece can become a convenient, timely reference and an instant wall hanging. You may prefer to do a square piece as your sampler, which could become a pillow, a

Sampler by Mary Ann Lee, Richmond, Va., 1826, worked on linen. Courtesy of The New-York Historical Society, New York City.

book cover, or a new sewing bag for yourself. If you are very brave and something of a seamstress (in addition to wanting to learn crewel embroidery), a long skirt with rows of border stitches and circles and squares of open and close filling stitches would be both stunning and functional. However, you may want to work up to such an ambitious undertaking. On the whole, it is often better for a beginner to start with something simple and moderate in size rather than a monumental project that could grow into such a monstrous task that it is left unfinished. Thus, the abrupt ending of your potential enjoyment of crewel.

Whatever the shape you choose, you should then select the design for your sampler. A square piece of fabric can be worked in a series of small squares, each filled with a different stitch. This is easily accomplished by dividing the piece of material into as many squares as stitches that you plan to practice. For example, if you plan to embroider twenty stitches, divide your fabric into twenty squares. A reliable method of obtaining equal squares is to fold the fabric in half lengthwise and then fold it again and again crosswise until you have the suitable number of spaces. Gently pressing the folds with your iron will produce more permanent guidelines. An explanation of how to apply a design to fabric appears in Chapter 5, if you think you would work more comfortably with marked lines on the fabric. Rather than marking the lines, but better than pressing them, you could stitch your guidelines onto the fabric in one of the simpler stitches, such as the running or stem stitch. A more casual adaptation of the filled-squares idea is merely to leaf through the pages that offer instructions for the stitches and experiment to your heart's content. In either case, you can always plan the placement of the stitches on paper—either in squares or scattered hither and yon—before taking needle and yarn in hand. These suggestions provide a guide to follow but are by no means unchangeable. If you find that you would like to combine two stitches that you had not previously considered

Sampler by Elisabetha S. Jephan, United States, 1844, worked on linen. Courtesy of The New-York Historical Society, New York City.

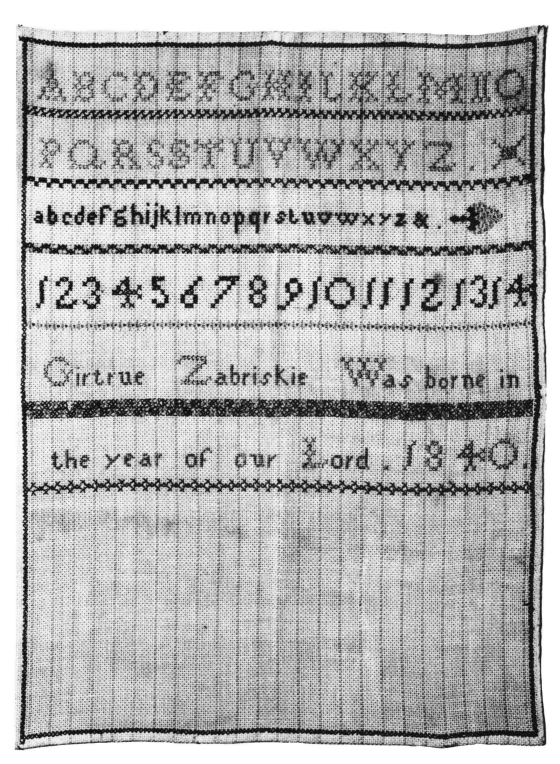

Sampler by Girtrue Zabriskie, United States, circa 1850, worked on homespun linen. Courtesy of The New-York Historical Society, New York City.

together, do not hesitate to rearrange your stitches, for you can always remove any work with which you find you are dissatisfied.

Another design suggestion is to work all the close filling stitches on one half of the fabric and all the open filling stitches on the other half of the fabric. In other words, work a few rows of the Rumanian stitch, the satin stitch, and the long and short stitch on the left-hand side or the upper half of the material, and work the opposite half of the fabric in a scattering of French knots, cloud filling, and seeding. Although this design does not give you as much practice in combining stitches, you can still experiment with color and thicknesses of yarn. Where it is feasible, sew one row of each stitch in one color, the next row in two shades of the color, and the third row in two different colors. Be sure to work both large and small stitches so that you can see how size affects the "flavor" of each stitch.

Geometric shapes worked in border stitches and filled with close filling stitches also produce an interesting and challenging sampler. This design requires some planning but gives you that much-needed practice in combining stitches, thicknesses of yarn, and color, which is one of the objects of your sampler.

Having decided upon the shape and the design of your work, all that remains to be done before the actual stitching is purchasing the basic materials. Most of the necessary supplies have been discussed in Chapter 1. For your sampler I would suggest that you buy between a half and a full yard of fabric (depending upon the shape and size of your project), a package of embroidery needles, a package of tapestry needles, a frame, and yarn. In choosing the yarn, try to limit yourself to a few colors and at least two shades of the color that you intend to use predominantly. This keeps the expense of the sampler to a minimum (to be boringly practical for a moment), and more important, creates a color theme in the work. Despite my endorsement of the use of vibrant colors in crewelwork, too much of a good thing can ruin the entire effect of almost anything, and embroidery is no exception. Select one color, which will become the dominant force, and choose the other colors as complements. A very brilliant color treated as the accent in a selection of soft colors often creates a very successful combination.

Selecting the shape, design, fabric, and colors of your sampler is really an exciting afternoon or evening's adventure. As you work and plan this piece, you may be "slapped in the face" with new ideas for your next project; or maybe not. But remember, if you are beginning from scratch, your first attempt at these stitches may not look exactly like the illustrations in this book. If they are unsatisfactory, you can always take the scissors to the yarn. So keep trying! This is a practice session, and it need not be letter-perfect. And above all, have fun while you are stitching.

Chapter 4
The History of Crewel Embroidery

To me one of the most charming qualities of a crewel embroidery piece is its history. Now that you have experimented with most of the stitches explained in Chapter 2, you may be interested in learning about the origins of crewelwork. If not, just skip this chapter. However, I found that the more involved I became with the history of crewel, the more fascinated I became with the entire subject.

The origin of the word "crewel" is unknown, although the most primitive form of the word, "crule," is thought to have been used in the fifteenth century. From "crule" the spelling evolved to "crewle," then to "crulle," "cruele," "croylle," "croole," "crewell," "cruel," and finally to the current version, "crewel." The *Oxford English Dictionary* defines "crewel" as "thin worsted yarn . . . of two threads, used for tapestry and embroidery." Therefore, crewel embroidery is that embroidery in which yarn is used to work the stitches.

Some of the first traces of crewelwork were found in England as early as Anglo-Saxon times. (The Anglo-Saxon migrations to England began in the middle of the fifth century A.D.) Later, approximately ten years after the Battle of Hastings (1066), one of the most famous pieces of embroidery, the Bayeux Tapestry, was designed to celebrate the Norman conquest of England; it is reputed to have taken ten years to stitch. Because the materials are so perishable, this is one of the few pieces of embroidery to have survived from this period. It is only because of repeated literary references in which the Normans express their admiration of such things as embroidered robes, tapestries, and vestments that we have learned of the existence of many pieces.

Ecclesiastical and historical embroidery continued into the thirteenth century. Typically, the whole surface of these pieces was covered with stitching. It is thought that the needles were made of wood, ivory, or slivers of bone.

Needless to say, the invention of the steel needle in England during the sixteenth century revolutionized stitchery! The prosperity and rich decoration that characterized these years were additional catalysts in transferring the practice of embroidery from the church into the home. It became quite stylish to have bedspreads, valances and curtains, pockets, wall hangings, and petticoats decorated with crewelwork. Domestic usage became so popular that wealthy enthusiasts often employed embroiderers or designers (or both) as part of the household staff. (Mary Queen of Scots, an avid needlewoman, was known to have had her own designers.)

Not that the popularity of embroidery was confined to the English court; it was already

Bed hanging: Tree of Life design embroidered in crewelwork, wool on cotton and linen twill. Late 17th century English. Courtesy of The Metropolitan Museum of Art, Rogers Fund, 1908.

coming to be a middle-class pursuit—so much so, that this sixteenth-century rage led to a real hunger for designs. Of course, in this era mass-circulation books did not exist, and the few pattern books that were published did not reach a very wide readership. To make matters worse, most of the pattern books at this time were printed in Italy, which added to the already considerable cost. Toward the end of the sixteenth century and into the early years of the seventeenth century a greater number of pattern books were published in England, but not in quantities sufficient to satisfy the demand. With books in such short supply, you would imagine that they would become cherished possessions, but, on the contrary, in what may to us seem a rather frivolous manner, the women of the sixteenth and seventeenth centuries often damaged the already scarce books by reproducing the patterns directly from the pages of the pattern book. From this scarcity of books the sampler emerged to fill the need for a permanent record of both the design and the stitches of various patterns, which were usually shared with friends and relatives.

Under the influence of the Stuarts, the popularity of crewelwork continued into the seventeenth century. English pieces made at this time have been dubbed Jacobean embroideries. A heaviness pervaded these designs, which had large spaces covered with close filling stitches. Later, Queen Anne's reign saw the introduction of lighter, more open patterns, frequently dotted with pineapples, florals, and scrolls.

Characteristically, these works used a variety of stitches: the outline, the rope, the cable (none of these is discussed in this book), the chain and its variations, the coral, and the couching for outlines, and the satin and the long and short for filling an area. Three motifs bloomed: 1) the tree of life; 2) the Elizabethan scroll (an arrangement of flowers enclosed by a number of sweeping stems that seemed to

Wall hanging: Tree of Life design hand painted on linen, late 17th or early 18th century. Courtesy of The New-York Historical Society, New York City.

Coverlet: "India Flower," worked in blue crewels on cream wool, fringed on three sides, Connecticut River Valley, 18th century. Courtesy of The Brooklyn Museum.

Seat cover: Wool on linen, 18th century American. Courtesy of The Metropolitan Museum of Art, Gift of Mrs. J. Insley Blair, 1946.

grow from one main stem); 3) the wavy border (developed later than the two others).

The Tree of Life pattern was inspired by the Indian palampores—cottons painted or printed with tropical flowers and fruits growing from one tree filled with animals and birds of lovely colorful plumage—brought back to the west by the great merchant traders. Additional influence came from the Persians, whose freedom and grace in floral designs were adapted for embroidery by the English designers. These Eastern traits were integrated with the Stuart emblems, such as the carnation, the oak leaf and acorn, and the caterpillar.

Coinciding with the flourishing of Jacobean embroidery, the first pieces of crewelwork were carefully carried to America by the colonists. Because wool was a valuable commodity and leisure time was limited in the early years of settlement, there was little or no handiwork done. The Puritan's distaste for decoration further hampered any efforts to embellish fabric with stitchery. However, the arrival of sheep about 1630 and the establishment of mills four years later by a group of weaving families from Yorkshire, England, changed this situation. Both fabric and yarn were made. Colonial women began to use natural dyes to tint their wool—indigo being the most widely used color at first. The pieces made in these early days were usually worked on homespun linen and in shades of indigo; these were the "blue and white" embroideries. Gradually the women learned to use the bark of walnut trees to make brown dye, leaves and twigs of sumac and goldenrod for yellow, pokeberry to produce purple tones, and finally, South American imported cochineal added to logwood for reds. Shades of colors were produced by controlling the number of dippings.

The initial ideas for early American designs came from England. Soon, however, pioneer women began to substitute the animals, fruits, and birds that surrounded them in their daily lives for the fantasylike flowers and birds of the palampores. Simplicity reigned in American crewelwork as the fancy foliage and complicated stitches were eliminated. Open designs with a special freshness developed; this must be largely attributed to the need to economize with wool. Stitches such as the economy, or flat, stitch, herringbone, running, or outline, French knots, buttonhole, and bullion knots were widely used, because most of these stitches are worked on the surface rather than through the back of the piece and are frugal in their use of yarn. The English habit of repeating motifs in the same piece virtually disappeared—probably because the American women both designed and embroidered the pieces themselves and soon came to know the type of design that was monotonous to sew.

Petticoats, pockets, chair seats, and pocketbooks were ornamented with stitches throughout the eighteenth century. Life became more civilized. Luxuries from different parts of the world appeared sporadically on the shelves of town shops. Among the array of imported items the wealthy needlewoman could be sure to find yarn and fabric. Ladies who found themselves with leisure time passed many an afternoon with a group of friends over their embroidery frames. Whether in a village classroom or a private school in the city, young girls from every walk of life were taught stitchery and their ABCs in the same classroom. Schools even advertised sewing as part of the curriculum. Crewel embroidery had evolved into a recreational art form from its previous utilitarian status; the golden age of needlework had established itself.

The height of crewel's popularity was cut short by the outbreak of the Revolutionary War, which forced women to abandon their embroidery hoops. This inevitable thrust away from handwork for handwork's sake was a blow from which crewelwork has yet to recover. After the war a quicker technique of covering fabric with stitches was employed. The custom of decorating bedspreads and hangings became unpopular, and only such small items as bonnet strings and bags were embroidered. Strands of

Curtain: part of a set of bed hangings. Red wool embroidered on cotton, done in outline stitch, blanket stitch, and seed stitch. Late 17th century American or English. Courtesy of The Metropolitan Museum of Art, Rogers Fund, 1940.

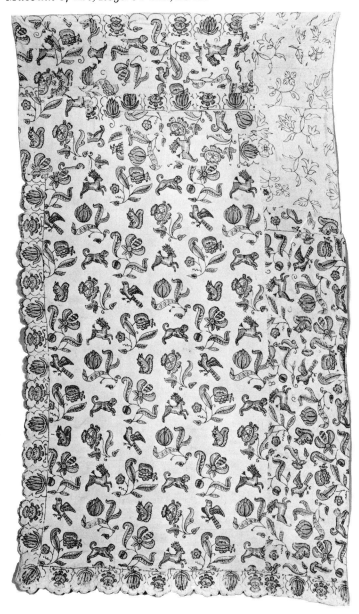

Bedspread: crewelwork, American, 1772. Courtesy of The Brooklyn Museum, gift of the Misses Latimer.

Detail of bedspread (showing upper middle-left)

Detail of bedspread (showing lower right)

Detail of bedspread (showing lower left)

yarn were replaced with silk threads as designs took on a decided change in tone. Gone was the former freehand grace; patterns became more geometric and harsh. The invention of the cotton gin during Washington's presidency crushed any chance that crewelwork might have had to regain its former popularity. With inexpensive decorated fabrics available, no one needed or wanted to spend time embroidering.

For more than half a century interest in embroidery remained dormant. Not until the late 1800s did a revival movement start in New England. The English once again played a decisive role in the level of American concern with crewelwork: the urging of William Morris, the poet, designer and artist, inspired the establishment of the Needlework School of the Museum of Fine Arts in Boston in 1879. The specific purpose of this school was to revive classic crewel embroidery as an art form. Shortly thereafter (in 1896) the Deerfield Blue and White Society was organized. The members found that their appreciation of crewelwork grew to such a degree that they were not satisfied with the colors of yarn and the linen they could purchase, and instead made their own linen and dyed their own yarn. Other organizations mushroomed across the country.

A variety of factors—World War I, the Depression, World War II, and perhaps an overreaction to the Victorian household—diverted interest away from handwork in the first half of the twentieth century. From that time on, we have witnessed an enormous self-sustaining buildup of the popularity of crafts—crewelwork among them. Yarn and thread companies that struggled for survival have become profitable; designers of needlework have become household names; craft classes have become crowded; and bookstores have devoted whole shelves to craft books. We are living through an era in which interest in handcrafts is at a peak. I, for one, encourage all who are the slightest bit interested in the creation of things beautiful to participate.

Coverlet: detail, Sarah Noyes Chester, Wethersfield, Conn., 18th century. Worked in wool on linen. Courtesy of The Metropolitan Museum of Art, gift of Mr. and Mrs. Frank Coit Johnson, through their son and daughter, 1944.

Blanket: by Ruth Brewster, embroidered in delft blue wool on undyed wool. 19th century American. Courtesy of The Metropolitan Museum of Art, Rogers Fund, 1928.

Chapter 5
Applying and Enlarging the Design

Once, peering into the window of a needlework shop, I overheard a woman nearby say to her companion, "Now, that's the sort of design I'd like to do in crewel, but I don't have any idea how to put it on the linen." I hope this chapter will provide the answers to similar questions that you may have. Once you have caught the crewel bug and want to embroider your own designs, applying them to the fabric is the next order of business. Before explaining the actual methods of enlarging and transferring a design to linen, I would like to suggest a few sources of inspiration, in case you are one of those people who doesn't think she could ever embroider an "original" because she can't draw.

Creating a design from the thoughts and visions in your mind's eye and reproducing it on paper requires a talent which is not second nature to everyone. People who do possess this ability are lucky indeed. However, in my opinion you do not have to be an artist to embroider your own designs. In the first place, part of the originality of a piece of embroidery is in selecting the colors and arranging the stitches. As discussed in the previous chapters, this takes practice and concentration. Second, being inspired by the world and objects around you and interpreting these ideas in embroidery certainly qualifies as original work. This was the technique adopted by the early American em-

broiderers when they severed their ties with the English designers of the seventeenth century. Furthermore, the surviving pieces from these early times have been a source of inspiration for many designs that are being embroidered today. There is no reason why you cannot use them yourself.

One of the most convenient places to begin your search for sources of inspiration is in your own home. Raid your linen closet. Examine your tablecloths, towels, and sheets for adaptable designs. Possibly you may see a geometric design emerge from the treasured but little-used tablecloth that your grandmother crocheted years ago. One of your dish towels may have a design on it that would brighten up your kitchen if you translated it into crewel. Wander through the rooms of your house and take a new look at the draperies, pictures, rugs, and wallpaper. One motif in any of these places could be singled out and transformed into a coordinating pillow. Your silk scarves and your child's old drawings are other potential sources.

Having gleaned all that you can from your home, you might next turn to nature and other objects out of doors. Nature itself provides one of the most obvious and most common sources of designs. You may even decide to invest in one of those guidebooks to flowers, trees, or birds which are available in most bookstores. You might visit an art gallery or museum to search for ideas. The postcard section in a museum gift shop could be an invaluable aid if you want to reproduce one of the great masterpieces in crewel. Greeting cards and wrapping paper often have interesting patterns that might spark your interest. A wealth of inspiration is found in a yard-goods store too.

After you have found a design—whatever the inspiration—and selected the stitches and colors, you are ready to cut your fabric to the desired size. Before you make the first cut in your material, always consider the intended use of the finished article, and be sure to allow extra material on all four sides of the design (⅝ inch should be sufficient) for seams. It may seem wasteful, but it is sound practice to leave an additional half inch around the design to allow a margin for error and to be certain that you have enough material to make the seam. You can always trim away excess fabric, but you can never add more material that won't show on the front of your embroidery. If, for example, the dimensions of your finished design, including the seam allowance, are 14 inches by 14 inches, cut the material 15 inches by 15 inches. In addition, I highly recommend that you stay-stitch all four sides of the fabric approximately one-quarter inch from the edge to help to prevent fraying. (Stay-stitching is a row of small machine stitches.)

The simplest method of transferring the design from the paper to the fabric is using dressmaker's carbon paper, or tracing paper, as it is often called. This paper is treated to assure a minimum of smudging, whereas regular typewriter carbon paper will smear all over you as well as your fabric. Dressmaker's carbon is readily available from any fabric or department store that sells sewing notions. Tracing paper is produced in a number of colors—white and blue being the most common. It would be wise to purchase a package of multicolored sheets, if this is available, because you should use a light-

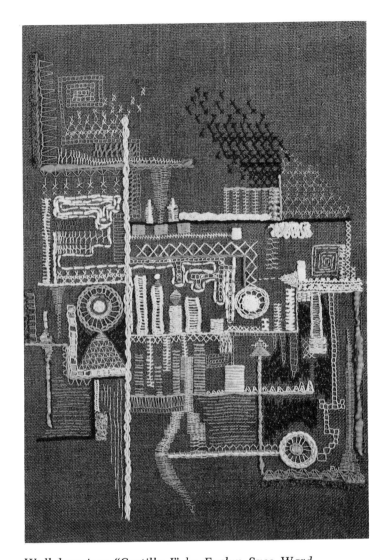

Wall hanging: "Castillo I" by Evelyn Svec Ward. Inspiration for this work came from a bamboo structure called a castillo, *which is erected for the Mexican fiesta; it is then lighted and explodes into a beautiful array of shooting and whirling colors. Worked in wool, cotton, metallic and mixed threads on burlap, in reds, oranges, and yellows on charcoal burlap, using various cross stitches, darning stitch, ladder stitch, chain stitch, open chain stitch, various buttonhole stitches, Vandyke stitch, Cretan stitch, various stem stitches, and couching stitch. Courtesy of Mrs. William H. Brisbin, Hudson, Ohio.*

colored paper to apply a design onto dark fabrics and a dark-colored paper for transferring onto light fabrics. You will also need masking tape, a straight pin, an empty ballpoint pen, a sharp pencil or a metal knitting needle to transfer the design, and a smooth, flat, hard surface upon which to work. Although it may sound trite to stress the working surface, it is important to transfer the design on a surface that has no bumps or ruts that could distort your outline. Some small weights (either a few paperweights or some small books will do) should be handy to hold the fabric in place as you apply the design. The steps involved in this method are the following:

1. Find the center of your fabric by folding the material in half twice, once lengthwise and once crosswise. Crease each fold by running your thumb and forefinger along it. If the fabric does not hold a crease well, baste two lines of stitches at the center of the material, one transecting it vertically, one horizontally. Use a contrasting color of thread for the basting stitches so that they are prominent. Fasten the material to your working surface with the masking tape. The wrong side of the fabric should be against the table. Be sure the fabric is smooth and firmly in place.

2. Trace or sketch your design on a piece of paper, making certain that it is in the center of the paper. Fold the design in the same manner as you folded the material to find the center. Crease the folds.

(ENLARGED) STRAIGHT PIN

DRESSMAKER'S CARBON PAPER (FACE DOWNWARDS)

PAPER WITH THE DESIGN ON IT

3. Put the dressmaker's carbon paper (face downward) underneath the design paper. With the straight pin, pierce the design paper and the carbon paper in the center. Push the pin through both layers of paper.

4. Holding the papers together in your left hand and guiding the pinhead with your right hand, put the point of the pin in the center of the fabric. Rotate the design and the carbon paper around the point so that the edges of the design and the material match or (if the design and fabric are of different sizes) are parallel. The design will now be centered. Check again to be positive that the carbon paper is face down against the material. Remove the straight pin and put your small weights around the edges of the material to hold the carbon paper and

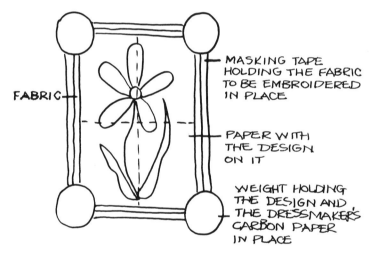

FABRIC

MASKING TAPE HOLDING THE FABRIC TO BE EMBROIDERED IN PLACE

PAPER WITH THE DESIGN ON IT

WEIGHT HOLDING THE DESIGN AND THE DRESSMAKER'S CARBON PAPER IN PLACE

the design in place. If you prefer to tape the pieces in place, you may. However, I advise using the weights so that you can check the progress of the transferring more readily. You will want to be sure that you are applying enough pressure to make a consistent line, and it is less trouble to lift a light weight than to have to untape an entire corner of your design.

5. Follow the outline of the design with your pencil, empty pen, or knitting needle. (My

experience with a knitting needle has taught me that a double-pointed needle is a very good tool. Because it is shorter than most regular knitting needles, it is much easier to control.) Do not make the line too broad, for it will be difficult to conceal it with yarn. One of the most disheartening things to see is a piece of crewelwork with the design guidelines showing through the stitching. After you have completed a portion of the design, lift a corner of the paper to inspect the results of your work. If you discover a line that is not distinct, go over that portion of your design applying heavier pressure.

One of the shortcomings of this method is that the markings of the design may rub off in some sections if the fabric is handled considerably while it is being embroidered. This can be avoided by very lightly spraying the fabric with a clear acrylic fixative, which you can purchase in an art-supply store. You should practice spraying a scrap of fabric with the fixative so that you do not squirt too heavy a coat on your piece.

The traditional and by far the most complicated method of applying the design is the pricking method. A type of stencil, the pricking is made by piercing the paper on which the design is pictured with a sharp instrument, and then rubbing a powder onto this paper through the holes so that a dotted outline appears on the fabric underneath. This is followed by going over the dots on the fabric with water-color paint to produce a solid outline. The required supplies include a long hatpin or a large safety pin, heavy tracing paper, a piece of tissue paper, a thick, soft piece of fabric or felt (slightly larger than the size of your work), to be used as a cushion on which to do the pricking, masking tape, a pouncer, pounce, a water-color brush with a fine point, a tube of blue or white (depending upon the color of fabric being used) water-color paint, and some light weights.

If you do not have a long hatpin, your first priority should be to make your pricking instrument. Simply purchase a large safety pin and bend it open. Next, you should think about your pouncer. You will use the pouncer to rub the pounce powder through the perforated paper with the design on it. A felt blackboard eraser will do very well. Or you could make a pouncer from flannel or felt. Roll a piece of felt or flannel very tightly and sew the roll together at each end. Pounce powder may be purchased in an art-supply store or a shop that sells embroidery supplies, or you can make some yourself by mixing nonscented talcum powder and powdered charcoal together. Both items are readily obtainable at a drugstore; most art-supply stores also carry powdered charcoal.

1. Before you begin pricking, sketch or trace your design onto the heavy tracing paper. Be certain the design is centered on the paper.
2. Lay your thick, soft fabric or felt flat on the table. Put the design face up on top of the cushioning fabric. Holding the pricking instrument directly perpendicular to the paper, prick holes through the tracing paper around the outline of the design. The holes should be very close together, especially in intricate parts of the design. You may use this pricking to transfer the design onto the fabric.

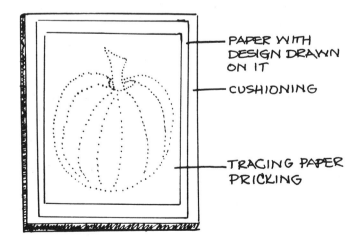

PAPER WITH DESIGN DRAWN ON IT

CUSHIONING

TRACING PAPER PRICKING

3. Find the center of both the pricking and the fabric to be embroidered by the method described in the section explaining the application of a pattern to the fabric by using dressmaker's carbon paper (page 79). Lay the fabric (front side up) on your flat working surface. Smooth the edges. Tape this fabric securely to the working surface. You will notice that one side of the pricking is rougher than the other. Place the smooth side of the pricking next to the material. Put light weights around the edges of the pricking to hold it in place.

4. Put the pounce into a shallow dish. Dip the pouncer into the pounce and shake off the excess. Working with a light circular motion, rub the pounce through the holes

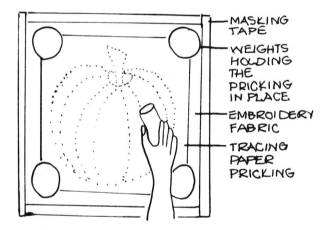

of the pricking onto the fabric underneath. Lift a corner of the pricking in order to make sure that the dots are coming through dark enough to act as a guide. When you have completed this step to your satisfaction, remove the pricking. If you find that there is any extra powder remaining on the fabric, carefully blow it away. This will assure you of a clear-cut line.

5. Mix the paint with water. You will do well to experiment with your mixture on a scrap of fabric to test the consistency of the paint. If the paint mixture is too watery, it will

run into the fabric and the outline of the design will become blurry. Paint an outline over the dots left by the pounce, again taking care to paint as thin a line as possible. Start at the edge that is closest to you, and put a piece of tissue paper over your finished

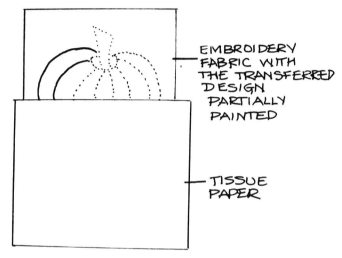

work. This will prevent you from smudging the painted lines. A ball-point pen may be substituted for the water-color paint and brush. However, the ink must be waterproof, or it will run during the blocking process. Test it by marking with the pen on a scrap of material and washing the material in water.

6. Let the fabric dry completely before you start to embroider on it.

A third technique in applying a design to a fabric is the use of basting stitches to make the outlines of the design. This is especially effective in preventing damage to a delicate fabric and becomes the essential method when working with knitted woolens—such as a sweater—on which it is impossible to trace or paint an accurate line. Perhaps the only disadvantage to this technique is that too complicated a design becomes difficult to follow.

You will need a piece of tissue paper or a lightweight material (organdie or chiffon will do very nicely), straight pins, a pencil, a sewing needle, and cotton thread. The thread should be of a color that contrasts with the color of the fabric, so that the basting stitches will be obviously distinguishable while you are embroidering over them.

1. Trace the design onto the tissue paper or the lightweight material with the pencil.
2. Pin the tissue paper or the lightweight material to the inside, or the wrong side, of the object that you plan to embroider exactly where you want to make your stitches. If your design is asymmetrical, you will have to put the tissue paper on the lightweight fabric face down against your article to be embroidered. Otherwise your design will become a mirror image of itself.

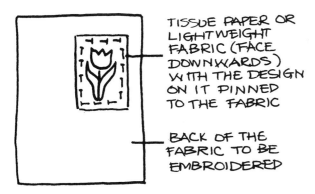

TISSUE PAPER OR LIGHTWEIGHT FABRIC (FACE DOWNWARDS) WITH THE DESIGN ON IT PINNED TO THE FABRIC

BACK OF THE FABRIC TO BE EMBROIDERED

3. Baste around the outline of the design (through both layers of fabric or through the fabric and the tissue paper) in a running

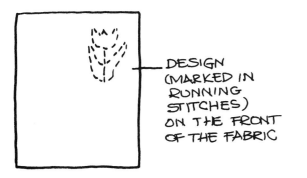

DESIGN (MARKED IN RUNNING STITCHES) ON THE FRONT OF THE FABRIC

stitch. The design will appear on both the front and the back of the piece which you are embroidering. Baste the edges of the fabric or tissue paper with the design on it to the fabric you plan to embroider. Remove the straight pins. This will prevent the pins from damaging the delicate embroidery material and from sticking you when you pick up your work!

4. Turn the fabric with the right side up and embroider the design on top of the running stitches. After you have finished the piece, you may trim away any excess lightweight material from the back. If you have used tissue paper, tear the paper away from the running stitches before you begin to embroider.

You may discover a design that you would like to adapt to embroidery, but would prefer to change the size. This problem may be easily solved without having to labor over mounds of paper tediously enlarging or reducing the design. If you are lucky enough to have a photocopy or xerographic service in your town, you can use this inexpensive and convenient method to alter the size of your design. Simply take the design to the service center and tell the operator what dimensions you want the reproduction to be. The next step is to trace the design onto tracing paper and apply it to your fabric. You may use any of the previously mentioned methods to transfer your design to the embroidery fabric, for as you can see, the design is now the correct size and can be treated as any other pattern you may want to embroider.

There is another technique you can use to enlarge or reduce a design; this is simply squaring off the design and reproducing the details within each square to the desired scale. Surprisingly enough, this is not as difficult as it sounds. The real prerequisites are patience and time. Whether you are working from large to small or small to large, the principle is the same.

1. With a ruler divide your design into squares. (If you do not want to write on the design directly, trace the pattern onto some tracing paper, so that you won't harm the original.) The number of squares is immaterial, but they must be equal in size. If you have a very tiny original, it could be divided into as few as twenty-five squares; a larger design could be squared into one hundred spaces.

2. Cut a piece of paper to the dimensions desired, excluding the seam allowance.

3. Whether you are reducing or enlarging a design, divide this paper into the same number of squares as appear in your original design. See the accompanying illustration.

4. Draw the details of each square of the original design into the corresponding squares of the enlargement or the smaller version of the design.

5. Proceed with any of the suggested techniques of applying this design to the fabric to be embroidered. If you find that the squares are now distracting, you may wish to retrace the design onto another piece of paper before beginning the embroidery.

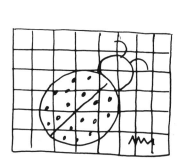

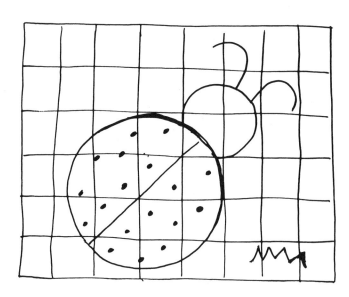

Chapter 6
Pressing, Blocking and Stretching

Having completed the stitching on what may be the first piece of embroidery that is entirely your own from the design to the color scheme to the stitch selection, you are now ready to add the finishing touches to your work. Whether you intend to make the embroidery into a pillow, a wall hanging, a chair seat, or an article of clothing, you must first eliminate the inevitable wrinkles that the piece acquired while it was being stitched. If you did most of your work with the fabric held tightly in a frame, this will be a matter of simple pressing, because the creasing should be minimal. However, if you stitched without a frame, the wrinkling is likely to be more extensive, and you will have to wet, block, and stretch the embroidery.

Although the blocking and stretching technique is time-consuming, it is the preferable method for most pieces, especially those embroidered on a heavy fabric. This procedure takes out every small wrinkle and crease, which pressing sometimes fails to do. Occasionally, pressing a piece of embroidery distorts the shape; blocking and stretching your work will cause it to hold its original shape. On the other hand, there are definite types of embroidery that cannot be blocked and stretched but must be pressed. Articles of clothing such as a wool sweater, a vest or a jacket, and pieces of embroidery having a fringed border fall into this category. If the edges of your work are to be exposed when it is finished, you will certainly not want the holes left by the carpet or upholstery tacks used in the blocking process to show; this kind of piece should be pressed.

As you can see, both methods of removing the wrinkles from your work have their advantages and disadvantages. The appropriate technique should be applied to each piece. Keep these things in the back of your mind as you embroider, so that you will not complete your place mats, for example, and find that they are too creased to use at the dinner table despite all your efforts with the iron.

When you press a piece of embroidery, do not apply too much pressure with the iron. Heavy-handedness will only crumple and flatten the stitches in your piece. A light touch is the best approach when you iron embroidery. Pressing your work on very thick padding also helps to prevent the stitches from being crushed. The procedure is as follows:

1. Place a thick, soft padding on the ironing board. A folded blanket or some towels will do.
2. Put the embroidery face down on the padding. This again will help to avoid crumpling the stitches.
3. Lay a damp cloth on top of the embroidery.

Wall hanging: "Primitive Islands" by Evelyn Svec Ward, 1960. Worked in tan, gray, red, and black wool on natural linen, using stem stitch, various chain stitches, the French knot, and buttonhole filling stitch. Courtesy of Container Corporation of America. Photo by William E. Ward.

4. Carefully and gently press the embroidery until it is wrinkle-free.

5. Proceed with the finishing plans. If you do not plan to mount the piece immediately, store the article around a cardboard roll to avoid creasing. A paper-towel roll is perfect for this. Wrap the embroidery around the tube with the stitches facing outward, so that they will not be crushed. You may want to wrap tissue paper around the roll to guard against dirt and dust. A pressed sweater or other embroidered article that cannot be stored around a cardboard tube should be kept on a hanger until you are ready to wear it.

To block and stretch your embroidery, you will need some supplies, which you should assemble before you begin to work: a board or working space a little larger than the embroidered piece, a hammer, carpet or upholstery tacks, and a sheet. (Warning: You will be hammering tacks into the board, so do not plan to use your coffee table.)

1. Cover the working space or board with the sheet.

2. Wet the embroidery thoroughly with cold water. The bathtub or a large laundry sink is the best place to douse the piece, because there you can open it out flat and soak it evenly.

3. Put the wet embroidery on the board or working space. If the piece has been embroidered with the relief stitches, such as French knots, etc., place the work with the front side upward, so that the stitches will not be crushed against the board. To obtain a flat finish on a piece that does not have raised stitches, put the front of the embroidery next to the sheet.

4. Tack the four corners of the piece to the board or working space, stretching the piece tightly into shape as you hammer. The four corners must be precise right angles or the shape of the piece will be distorted. Do not be afraid to tug on the material.

5. Nail four more tacks into the fabric, one in the center of each side. Continue to pull the material taut.

6. Nail eight tacks in the spaces created by step 5. Again keep the fabric tightly stretched.

7. Continue to hammer tacks in this fashion around all four sides of the embroidery until the tacks are approximately a quarter of an inch apart. Be sure to balance each tack with one on the opposite side.

8. Let the embroidery dry completely. Remove the tacks—and you are ready to make up the piece of embroidery into its final form. As suggested in step 5 of the instructions concerning pressing a piece of embroidery, store your project around a cardboard roll if you do not plan to work with it immediately. If the piece has been embroidered with raised or textured stitches, wrap it so that the stitches are facing outward. If there is likely to be a long storage period, tissue paper or a plastic bag should also be wound around the embroidery to keep the piece clean.

Chapter 7
Projects

WRIST PINCUSHION

A wrist pincushion is not only simple to make but is also an extremely useful project. Possibly you will find, as I did, that keeping your various-size needles handy while you embroider is somewhat of a necessity. Sticking the needles in the arm of a padded chair is not a good habit to develop. This I rather abruptly learned one day when I forgot to remove the needles from the arm of the chair before my husband sat down in it. For me a wrist pincushion became an absolute must.

Materials: tracing paper or tissue paper, yarn, embroidery needle, fabric, ½-inch-wide elastic, stuffing (small pieces of cotton or cotton balls are excellent), cotton thread of a color to match the fabric, sewing needle, and straight pins.

1. Select a design that is no larger than 2 inches in diameter. The example is worked in an abstract design of two stitches; you may prefer to embroider something animate. Remember that there is a tiny working space, so keep the design uncomplicated.

2. Make the pattern for your pincushion from the tissue or tracing paper by cutting a 3-inch square out of the paper. (This includes a ⅝-inch seam allowance.) Pin the pattern to the fabric. Cut out the square. Remove the pattern from the square.

3. Pin the pattern to another section of the fabric and cut out a second square. These will be the front and back pieces of your pincushion. Stay-stitch the pieces.

4. Apply the design to the piece of the fabric that will be the front of the pincushion.

5. Stitch the design.

6. Because the piece is quite small, it would be best to press the embroidery.

7. Measure a ⅝-inch seam allowance around all four sides of both the front and back pieces of fabric. Mark the seams with pins. Press the seams to the insides of both pieces.

8. With the right, or front, sides of both pieces of fabric face to face, pin three sides of the two pieces of fabric together.

9. Using tiny stitches (or a sewing machine if you have one), sew the seams together on the three sides of the square with cotton thread. Trim the seams to within ¼-inch of the stitches. Clip the corners diagonally. Turn the square right side out.

10. Shred the cotton and cotton balls. Carefully stuff the pincushion until the square is snugly packed, making certain that the corners are full.

11. Stitch the opening closed with cotton thread.

12. Measure a piece of elastic to fit your wrist, add one inch, and cut the piece of elastic. Turn the elastic under twice—¼ inch each time—at each end. Stitch the hems with the cotton thread.

13. Pin each turned-under end to an opposite

side of the pincushion (with the design uppermost), forming a bracelet. Then stitch the elastic to the cushion. Remove the pins.

PILLOW

You have probably realized that the pincushion is simply a pillow on a small scale. Try a round or rectangular pillow; the principles are the same. Simply follow the procedure in steps 1 through 11, with the exception of step 6. In this case you may prefer to block and stretch your pillow rather than press it. Remember to include seam allowances in the dimensions of your pillow. Nylon stockings make a good stuffing for pillows, so start saving those with runs in them and ask your friends to do the same. Or you can use a commercially made pillow form. (These forms are sold in specific dimensions, so choose a size and keep these dimensions in mind as you plan the design for your pillow.)

Tassels make a festive trim for many pillows. To attach a tassel to the pillow, insert the end of the tassel into the corner of the pillow (from the right side) as you pin the seams of the pillow together in step 8. Then stitch the tassel in place at the same time as you stitch the seams together in step 9. Make a few extra stitches in each corner to be certain that the tassel is secure. To make a tassel:

1. Cut six or eight 36-inch lengths of yarn. Cut two 9-inch lengths of yarn.
2. Assemble all the 36-inch lengths in one bunch, making certain that the ends are even.
3. Fold the yarn in half twice; the pieces are now about 9 inches long. Cut through the folds at both ends.
4. Tie the bunch of clipped yarn together in the center very tightly with one of the 9-inch lengths of yarn. Tie six or eight loose square knots in this 9-inch length.

5. Fold the yarn bunch in half again so that the square-knotted 9-inch length is at the top of the tassel. The tassel is now approximately 4½ inches long.
6. Tie the second 9-inch length around both halves of the tassel, approximately one-third of the length of the tassel from the top. Tie a few extra knots to be certain that the yarn is secure.
7. Trim the ends of the tassel.

Note: If you prefer a fatter or a thinner tassel, simply increase or decrease the number of 36-inch strands you use.

CHAIR-SEAT COVER

One of the most frequently made pieces of crewelwork, a chair-seat cover offers a splendid opportunity to display your stitching talents. You may own a chair or a set of dining-room chairs that need to be recovered; this is an inexpensive and enjoyable way to do it.

Materials: yarn, fabric, embroidery needle, frame, tissue paper or tracing paper, straight pins, upholstery tacks, hammer, and screw driver.

1. Select your design, color scheme, and stitches.
2. Remove the chair seat from the chair. Although it is difficult to make a general state-

Chair seat cover: Danish, "Anno 1903." Dark blue wool embroidery. Courtesy of The Brooklyn Museum.

ment about all dining-room chairs, usually this type of chair has four screws holding the seat in place. For the purpose of uniformity, I am assuming this is the type of chair that is being covered.

3. Remove the upholstery tacks and the old seat cover from the cushion form.

4. Press the old chair-seat cover so that the edges lie flat. Trace the outline of the old chair-seat cover onto the tracing or tissue paper. (You may have to tape two or three pieces of tracing paper together if you do not have large-size paper.) Pin this paper pattern to your fabric. Cut out the new chair-seat cover and stay-stitch it.

5. Apply your design to the fabric.

6. Stitch the design.

7. Block the finished chair-seat cover as suggested in Chapter 6.

8. When the embroidery is completely dry, you can mount the cover on the cushion form. Put the embroidery face downward on your flat working surface. Center the cushion form face downward on the embroidery. Attach the cover to the form by nailing four upholstery tacks through the form and the embroidery, one in each corner. (Nail the tacks in opposite corners as you do this, rather than in the two corners at the top and the two at the bottom. This will help to keep the fabric and the design from being pulled to one side.) To ensure that the embroidery will be wrinkle-free and well stretched when you are finished, pull the fabric tightly as you attach it. Hammer four more tacks along the four sides, one tack in the center of each side. Continue to hammer the tacks into the chair cushion form and the embroidery, one on the left side and one directly opposite on the right side, one along the top edge and one opposite along the bottom edge, until the tacks are approximately ¼ inch apart all the way around the cushion.

9. Attach the chair seat to the chair and have a seat!

SHOULDER BAG

Making a shoulder bag gives you a chance to wear your embroidery. Because purses and handbags have become such versatile accessories, you can really use your imagination and ingenuity in this project.

Materials: yarn, approximately one yard of fabric, embroidery needle, frame, straight pins, tissue paper or tracing paper, cotton thread to match the color of your fabric, sewing needle, approximately ¾ yard of lining fabric, string, ruler, and approximately ¾ yard of Pellon.

1. Select a design and choose the color scheme and stitches.

2. Make a pattern for the body of the shoulder bag from the tracing paper or the tissue paper. Decide how large you would like the bag to be; the example is 12 inches wide and 16 inches long. Add the seam allowance (⅝ inch) to all four sides. Calculate the total dimensions of the bag; the example is 13¼ inches wide and 17¼ inches long. Be very precise in your measurements and addition because this project will not include the ½-inch margin-for-error fabric. (See Chapter 5 for an explanation of this term.) Draw a rectangle the total dimensions of your bag (including seam allowances) on the tracing or tissue paper. Fold the paper in half and trim away the excess paper, rounding the bottom left and right corners if you wish. (By folding the paper in half before you cut it you are certain to obtain equally rounded corners.)

3. Make a pattern for the flap of the bag in

the same fashion. The flap should overlap the bag between one-third and one-half the distance from the top. The dimensions of the flap in the example would be 13¼ inches by 7¼ inches. If you prefer a bag that will hold more, put a gusset between the front and back pieces. You must then increase the length of the flap by the width of the gusset. There is a 2-inch gusset in the example; the flap measures 13¼ inches wide and 9¼ inches long. Draw a square the total size of the flap on the tracing or tissue paper. Fold the paper in half and trim away the excess. If you care to round the lower corners, do so.

4. Take the string and sling it over your shoulder as if it were the strap of a shoulder bag. Adjust the string to a comfortable shoulder-bag length, and mark the correct point by pinching the string with your thumb and forefinger. Remove the string from your shoulder and measure the length. Add a ⅝-inch seam allowance and 2 inches for overlap to each end, and record the total length. Select a width for your strap. (The example strap is 2 inches wide.) Add the ⅝-inch seam allowance for each side, and record the figure.

5. Fold the fabric in half and pin the pattern pieces (flap and bag) to the fabric. Be certain the pieces are straight and running with the lengthwise grain of the fabric. Cut around the outline of the pattern pieces through both thicknesses of the material. Stay-stitch these pieces.

6. Unfold the fabric. Cut a strip of material for the strap of the bag according to your recorded length and twice your recorded width, including the seam allowance. If you are making a gusset, cut it out as follows: measure the total distance around the outside of the bottom and the two sides of the bag, add ⅝-inch seam allowance to all measurements, and cut the strip.

7. Apply the design to the piece of fabric that will be the front of the flap and the front of the bag.

8. Stitch the design.

9. Block and stretch or press the embroidery.

10. Cut two bag pieces and a gusset from the lining fabric and the Pellon. Stitch the Pellon to the inside of the corresponding lining piece. Trim the Pellon very close to the stitches.

11. Measure and mark with a pin the ⅝-inch seam allowance along the top edges of all the pieces of the bag, flap, and gusset. Do the same with the lining. Press the seams to the inside of all pieces.

12. With right sides facing, pin the two flaps together along the three sides. Do not pin the top edge. Sew the three sides together. Do not stitch the top.

13. With right sides facing, pin the front and back of the bag to the gusset. Stitch the pieces together. Press these seams open.

14. Fold the strap in half, with the right sides facing. Pin the long side seam and one end together. Stitch the seams ⅝ inch from the edge. Trim the seam ¼ inch from your stitches. Clip the corners diagonally. Turn the strap right side out. Turn the seam allowance on the open end of the strap to the inside and stitch the end closed. Press the strap.

15. With right sides facing, pin the flap along the top edge of the back of the bag. Stitch a seam ⅝ of an inch from the edge.

16. With right sides facing, pin the front and back lining to the gusset lining. Stitch a ⅝-inch seam again. Press the seams open.

17. Keep the lining inside out and set it inside the bag. Be certain that the pressed seam allowances of both the lining and the bag are still toward the wrong side of both fabrics. Pin the lining in place ¼ inch from the top edge of the bag. Stitch the lining in place.

18. Pin the strap to the outside of the bag along the gusset, 2 inches from the top edge of the bag. Stitch the strap in place. If you do not have a gusset on your bag, attach the strap to the back of the bag next to the seam, 2 inches from the top edge.

WALL HANGING OR PICTURE

A crewel wall decoration is especially complementary to any room in your home—the den, study, a child's room, bathroom, or kitchen. Wall hangings may be interestingly hung like a scroll, with dowels at the top and bottom. Or you can make a picture (not hung in an ordinary frame) which is tacked to a piece of wood and trimmed in velvet ribbon.

Materials: yarn, embroidery needle, frame, fabric, and hanging equipment, depending on the project (wall hanging: a dowel that is the length of twice the width of your piece plus 2 inches; picture: a ¾-inch-thick piece of wood that is exactly the dimensions of your finished piece, ⅝-inch velvet ribbon of a color to complement your piece and long enough to go completely around it, glue, upholstery or carpet tacks, and hammer), cotton thread, and needle.

1. Select a design, color scheme, and stitches.
2. Choose the size of the piece; the example picture is 9 inches wide and 12 inches tall, and the wall hanging is 12 inches wide and 18 inches tall. If you are making a wall hanging, add 2 inches to the width of the piece for hem allowances (there will be a one-inch hem on each side) and 4 inches to the length for hem allowances (there will be a 2-inch hem top and bottom). If you plan to attach the piece to a block of wood, add 2 inches to all four sides.
3. Cut the fabric. Stay-stitch the piece.
4. Apply the design.
5. Stitch the piece.
6. Block and stretch the piece if it will be attached to the wood; press the piece if it is to be a wall hanging.
7. To make a wall hanging:
   (a) Fold the fabric to make a hem that folds over twice (½ inch each fold) along each side edge, so that the raw fabric is not visible.
   (b) Stitch the hems.
   (c) Turn the bottom and top edges under ½ inch and stitch the hems down.
   (d) Make a second hem, this time 1½ inches deep, on the top and bottom of the piece.
   (e) Saw the dowel exactly in half. (The store from which you purchase the dowel will probably cut it for you.) Slip the dowels into place. Each dowel will protrude approximately ½ inch from each of the four corners.
8. To make a picture:
   (a) Put the embroidery face down on the working surface. Center the wood block on it.
   (b) Attach the embroidery to the wood according to the directions in this chapter for attaching a chair-seat cover to a chair seat.
   (c) Glue the ribbon around the edges of the wooden block, now covered with the fabric.
   (d) If you prefer, you may make a backing for the picture. Cut another piece of fabric the size of your piece. Measure, pin, and press the seam allowance to the back side of the fabric. Place the backing fabric on the back of your picture and tack it in place with the upholstery or carpet tacks.

Concluding Remarks

Whether you select one of these projects as your first or whether you have an idea of your own to pursue, the most thrilling upshot of having completed your first piece will not be the actual embroidery itself, but rather the realization that you have created something completely personal and beautiful with your own hands; I find this a rare experience in today's mechanized society. The joy of watching a design virtually come alive as you stitch is part of the excitement of crewel embroidery. The personality and creativity of your crewel work comes entirely from you: you choose the materials and color scheme and execute the design and stitches. You are the only person who gives vivacity and originality to your work. And, I trust, you will enjoy yourself as well!

Apart from having the fruits of your stitching to admire and those of your mind to ponder, you will also have the satisfaction of knowing that you have taught yourself crewel embroidery merely by sitting down with needle and yarn in hand and actually practicing the stitches. As you experiment with more sophisticated combinations of stitches, more intricate designs, and various fabrics and yarns, you will find that the adage "Practice makes perfect" is in fact more than just a collection of words. It is my firm belief that anyone can do crewel embroidery if she or he cultivates the patience and takes the time to practice the craft. Once you have begun your sampler, you will discover just how easy stitchery really is! I reiterate what I have stressed in previous chapters: the first stitches may not be the same size or exactly perfect, but do not be discouraged—and above all, keep trying and practicing.

As your knowledge of crewel embroidery flourishes, you may soon be bursting with ideas for many different projects you would like to make. Most likely, the sources of your inspiration will become more varied as your scope widens. Perhaps you may find yourself thinking, "*That* would make a beautiful piece of crewel" before you realize you are doing it. Your eyes may be opened to a new manner of appreciating and enjoying paintings, photographs, and, indeed, everything around you in your search for design ideas for your embroidery.

Whatever you discover in your adventures with crewel embroidery, I do hope you enjoy making your contribution to the perpetuation of what I feel is a worthwhile revival of a lovely and traditional craft!

Sources of Supply

This is only a very partial listing of retail suppliers of crewel and embroidery materials. To find the names and addresses of likely sources of needlework supplies in your area, write to the companies listed below, or check the Yellow Pages under "Art Needlework Materials." Most larger department stores and craft shops have needlework departments. A listing entitled "Where to Buy Handwork Supplies" is available from McCall's for 25¢ (ask for Leaflet No. 804-NB).

Retail Stores

American Bequest Designs, 36 Oak Street, Southington, Conn. 06489

Bell Yarn, 75 Essex Street, New York, N.Y. 10002

Emile Bernat and Sons Co., Uxbridge, Mass. 01569

Betsy Ross Needlework, Inc., 2 Alsan Way, Little Ferry, N.J. 07643

Boutique Margot, 26 West 54th Street, New York, N.Y. 10019

Clicking Needles Studio, 104 Fifth Avenue, Suite 1806, New York, N.Y. 10011

Columbia-Minerva, 295 Fifth Avenue, New York, N.Y. 10016

Crain Harmon, 799 Broadway, New York, N.Y. 10003

The D.M.C. Corporation, 107 Trumbull Street, Elizabeth, N.J. 07206

Dritz, Scovill Mfg. Co., 350 Fifth Avenue, New York, N.Y. 10001

Fancywork, 1235 First Avenue, New York, N.Y. 10021

Frederick J. Fawcett, Inc., 129 South Street, Boston, Mass. 02111

Eric H. Greene and Co., 11044 Weddington Street, Box 257, North Hollywood, Calif. 91603

Hidden Glen, Meadowbrook, Pa. 19046

Knitters World, Inc., Manchester, Conn. 06050

Lion Brand Yarn Co., 1270 Broadway, New York, N.Y. 10001

The Little Red Schoolhouse, School Street at Sink Road, Route #4, Dowagiac, Mich. 49047 (P.O. Box 148)

Alice Maynard Needlepoint, 558 Madison Avenue, New York, N.Y. 10022

Mazaltov's, 758 Madison Avenue, New York, N.Y. 10021

The Merino Wool Co., Inc., 1140 Broadway, New York, N.Y. 10001

Needleloft, Mill Lane, Farmington, Conn. 06032

Needlepoint a la carte, 325 S. Woodward, Birmingham, Mich. 48011

Marion Nichols Needlework Originals, Inc., 71 Sylvester Street, Westbury, N.Y. 11590

Norden Needle Crafts, Box 1, Glenview, Ill. 60025

Orchard Yarn and Thread Co., 524 West 23rd Street, New York, N.Y. 10011

Paragon Needlecraft, 367 Southern Boulevard, Bronx, N.Y. 10454

Reynolds Yarns, Inc., 215 Central Ave., East Farmingdale, N.Y. 11735

Selma's Art Needlework, 1645 Second Avenue, New York, N.Y. 10028

Sew Simple, Inc., 710 Summa Avenue, Westbury, N.Y. 11590

The Sinkler Studio, 223 Iven Avenue, Radnor, Pa. 19087

Spinnerin Yarn Co., Inc., 230 Fifth Avenue, New York, N.Y. 10001

Titillations, Ltd., 211 East 60th Street, New York, N.Y. 10022

Tobin, Sporn & Glaser, 8 West 30th Street, New York, N.Y. 10001

Joan Toggitt, Ltd., 1170 Broadway, New York, N.Y. 10001

Bernhard Ulmann Co., 30-20 Thomson Avenue, Long Island City, N.Y. 11101

William Unger & Co., Inc., 230 Fifth Avenue, New York, N.Y. 10001

Unusual Imports, Lakeville, Conn. 06039

Elsa Williams Needlecraft, Inc., West Townsend, Mass. 01474

Erica Wilson Needle Works, 717 Madison Avenue, New York, N.Y. 10021

Yarn Kits, Inc., 361 East 50th Street, New York, N.Y. 10022

The Yarn Shop, 629 Arnold Avenue, Point Pleasant, N.J. 08742

Yarns Unlimited, 219 Wilshire Boulevard, Santa Monica, Calif. 90406

Mail Order Stores

(Many of thes stores will furnish catalogs on request.)

American Crewel and Canvas Studio, P.O. Box 1756, Point Pleasant Beach, N.J. 08742

American Handicrafts Co., Box 791, Fort Worth, Texas 76107

Crossroads, Box 418, North Hollywood, Calif. 91603

The Golden Eye, Box 205, Chestnut Hill, Mass. 02167

Greenfield Designs, Box 144, Greenfield, Ind. 46140

Heritage Hill Patterns, Box 624, Westport, Conn. 06880

Herrschners Needlecrafts, Hoover Rd., Stevens Point, Wis. 54481

"In" Stitches, Box 147, Miami, Fla. 33165

International Creations, 160 Cabot Street, West Babylon, N.Y. 11704

Katharine Knox, 445 Plandome Road, Manhasset, N.Y. 11030

Lee Wards, Elgin, Ill., 60120

Little Red Schoolhouse, School Street at Sink Road, Route #4, Dowagiac, Mich. 49047 (P.O. Box 148)

Mary Maxim, Inc., 2001 Holland Ave., Port Huron, Mich. 48060

Mazaltov's, 758 Madison Avenue, New York, N.Y. 10021

Merribee Co., Box 9680, Fort Worth, Texas 76107

Needlecraft House, West Townsend, Mass. 01474

Needles 'N Hoops, Box 165, Abington, Pa. 19001

Norden Needle Crafts, Box 1, Glenview, Ill. 60025

Perks' Packages, Box 10998, Jackson, Miss. 39209

Scandinavian Import Corp., Box 347, Madison Square Station, New York, N.Y. 10010

Sears Roebuck: Write to the district office nearest you for the "Sears Crafts Catalog."

Jane Snead Samplers, Box 4909, Philadelphia, Pa. 19119

The Stitchery, Wellesley, Mass. 02181

Stitchery Studio, 2 Bridge Street, Plattsburgh, New York 12901

Stitch Witchery, P.O. Box N, Denville, N.J. 07834

Sunray Yarn House, 349 Grand Street, New York, N.Y. 10002

Thumbelina Needlework Shop, 1688 Copenhagen Drive, Solvang, Calif. 93463

Erica Wilson Needle Works, 717 Madison Avenue, New York, N.Y. 10021

Yarns Unlimited, 219 Wilshire Boulevard, Santa Monica, Calif. 90406

Other Sources

Among the many needlecraft magazines currently available are:

Embroiderer's and Needlecrafter's Journal (published quarterly), 220 Fifth Avenue, New York, N.Y. 10001

Needle Arts (published quarterly by the Embroiderer's Guild of America, 120 East 56th Street, Room 228, New York, N.Y. 10022

The list of advertisers in these magazines can be checked for craft shops and needlework guilds in your area.

Finally, Simplicity Patterns has just come out with embroidery designs for crewelwork in the form of iron-on transfers, sold wherever Simplicity Patterns are sold.

Index of Stitches